SYSTEMS THEORY AND FAMILY THERAPY

A Primer

Raphael J. Becvar
Dorothy Stroh Becvar

UNIVERSITY
PRESS OF
AMERICA

LANHAM • NEW YORK • LONDON

Copyright ©1982 by **Raphael J. Becvar, Dorothy Stroh Becvar**

University Press of America,™ Inc.

4720 Boston Way
Lanham, MD 20706

3 Henrietta Street
London WC2E 8LU England

Printed in the United States of America

Library of Congress Cataloging in Publication Data

Becvar, Raphael J., 1931–
  Systems theory and family therapy.

  Includes index.
  1. Family psychotherapy. 2. Social systems. I.
Becvar, Dorothy Stroh. II. Title.
RC488.5.B39   616.89'156   81–43721
ISBN 0–8191–2443–5   AACR2
ISBN 0–8191–2444–3 (pbk.)

All University Press of America books are produced on acid-free
paper which exceeds the minimum standards set by the National
Historical Publications and Records Commission.

To John and Lynne Reif,
very important members
of our family system.

ACKNOWLEDGEMENTS

The persons most responsible for this book, other than ourselves, are those couples and families whom we have endeavored to help to experience happier lives with one another, and our students, whose provocative questions pushed us to think more clearly and to present the contents of this book more effectively. We are indebted to the seminal theoriests of the systems model and to the marriage and family theorists upon whose work we built. We owe a special debt of gratitude to Steven Bartlett, whose probing in the area of epistemological analysis challenged us to seek new levels of understanding. Ray is particularly appreciative of the ideas and guidance provided by Margaret Hoopes, A. Lynn Scoresby, and Robert Stahmann at Brigham Young University. Dee gives special thanks to Jo-Ann Pierie, Frank Toia, and their families, for providing a context of love, encouragement, and support at a most crucial point in her own family life cycle.

CONTENTS

...each man contemplates in his own
personal way the stream of events upon
which he finds himself so swiftly borne.

George Kelly

This book is designed to be used as an introduction to a systems epistemology. It does not pretend to be an all inclusive work. Rather, it seeks
to provide basic learning to stimulate the reader to learn more about systems,
about families, and about family therapy.

The reader is forewarned that we do not present the systems perspective.
We present a systems perspective--our perspective. We describe some of the
basic constructs by means of which social systems may be understood and we
then challenge the reader to use this information to build his or her own
theory about systems. This, we feel, one cannot not do. Indeed, it is
highly unlikely that any person ever totally comprehends or understands a
theory in exactly the same way as any other person. You may have your
comprehension of a theory, but it probably is not the same understanding as
that of its author. As we read any theory, we experience the meaning of its
constructs and concepts consistent with and dependent upon the framework of
concepts we have already learned.

The illustration and examples provided in this book as we seek to explain
concepts are based on the family as the social system of greatest interest to
us. We could have used other social systems as examples. However, a more
general application was not our purpose. You may find the concepts useful
as you seek to understand other systems, but we leave that application to
you.

In the chapter entitled, IMPLICATIONS FOR FAMILY THERAPY, we do not provide a comprehensive, detailed delineation of our approach. Rather, we describe some general propositions and ideas which we have inferred from our systems perspective. You might consider these propositions and ideas as you build your own model for working with families.

Marriage and family therapy as an activity has legitimacy only from a perspective that sees people as interdependent. It makes no sense to do marriage or family therapy if one sees people as independent agents. A systems perspective provides a way of understanding the dynamics of this interdependence.

Chapter 1

ABOUT THEORIES

> To be accepted as a paradigm, a theory must
> seem better than its competitors, but it need
> not, in fact never does, explain all the facts
> with which it can be confronted.
>
> Thomas Kuhn

To examine the developmental history of human societies is to learn of the many different ways in which people have attempted to explain the phenomena in their worlds. Kelly (1955) described all people as scientists seeking to understand, predict and control their worlds. Berrien (1968) spoke of mankind's interminable need to make sense out of experience by raising it to ever higher levels of abstraction as an "incurable disease." And the different explanations or theories offered and employed have each lead to courses of action different from those indicated by prior explanations or theories. Thus the explanation of the world as flat discouraged self-conscious attempts to sail around it. The explanation of "mental illness" as possession by demons suggested responses such as prayer, flagellation, or exorcism. Indeed, the course of action we take is bound up with the explanation or meaning we experience when we encounter an event. Different explanations produce different interpretations and feelings which interact with different kinds of responses.

While the meaning we experience is a functional "truth" for us, we are always reminded that the same event can be given many interpretations. We typically select that interpretation which we believe will best serve our purposes. Such an explanation is derived from our personal frame of reference and thus tends to validate the theory. A person who believes that people are weak will have a predisposition to look for evidence of weakness in

1

others. Thus we are usually able to accept a different theory only in the face of overwhelming evidence to the contrary which invalidates our prior explanation.

Each of us has several personal theories to explain physical, biological and interpersonal phenomena. Our personal theories are our guides as we move toward greater meaning and satisfaction in our lives. Such guides are maps; they are not the territory (Bateson, 1972). Most of us are aware of certain inadequacies in our personal theories. Therefore we often seek different, richer, or more detailed maps.

This book focuses on the family and offers a theory for your consideration. This theoretical perspective is derived from General Systems Theory as it has evolved vis-a-vis an attempt to understand the dynamics of families. The systems perspective has demonstrated its efficacy in the physical, biological, and social sciences; its application to the study of human beings has been equally fruitful.

The emergence of a systems perspective for families and its acceptance by a significant number of practitioners suggests that a change has occurred which represents a shift in paradigms. A paradigm is a coherent tradition or framework shared by a given scientific community. It refers to a whole realm of experience, including beliefs, values, and methodology, subscribed to by members of that community (Kuhn, 1970).

To many social scientists, systems theory seems better than its rivals, for it can explain and predict events and solve problems recognized by practitioners as acute. That the systems perspective has come into its own is indicated by the growing number of professional journals and societies concerned with this topic as well as by inclusion in university curricula. According to Kuhn (1970), these may all be considered characteristic of a paradigm shift.

There are many explanations for the emergence of systems theory as a new paradigm. Minuchin has offered an explanation which we find useful:

> Psychoanalysis is a nineteenth century concept....
> Its the product of a romantic idea of the hero and
> his struggle against society; it is about man out of
> context. Today we are in a historical period in
> which we cannot conceive of non-related things.
> Ecology, ethology, cybernetics, systems, structural
> family therapy are just different manifestations of a
> concern for the relatedness of our resources. Family
> therapy will take over psychiatry in one or two dec-

2

ades because it is about man in context. It is a
therapy that belongs to our century, while individual therapy belongs to the nineteenth century. This
is not a pejorative. It is simply that things evolve
and change, and during any historical period certain ways of looking at and responding to life begin
to crop up everywhere. Family therapy is to psy-
chiatry what Pinter is to theatre and ecology is to
natural science.(Malcolm, 1978, p.76)

The systems perspective is a universal view. It does not interpret events
in isolation from other events. Most of us acknowledge the interdependence
of physical, biological and social systems as well as the interdependence of
people within social systems. However, we often take courses of action intended to improve relationships which focus only upon individual members
of these systems, thus ignoring the reciprocal influence we have upon one
another. A systems perspective would focus our attention on individuals only in the context of their relationships, consistent with a framework of contextual relativity, and it would have us behave accordingly. As Whitehead
has noted, "a civilization which cannot burst through its current abstractions
is doomed to sterility after a very limited period of progress" (Whitehead,
1926, p. 26).

Chapter 2

SYSTEMS THEORY: A PARADIGM SHIFT

> The theory will have shown its value if
> it opens new perspectives and viewpoints
> capable of experimental and practical
> application.
>
> Ludwig von Bertalanffy

At base, the concept of a system is an invention which is used to describe regularities or redundant patterns we observe between people and other phenomena. Thus, systems exist only as we give them existence by observing regularities or patterns. It is useful and simplifies our understanding of the world to conceptualize a given pattern of relationships as a system.

Let us emphasize again our belief that the concept of a system, systems theory, or a systems perspective is, like all other theories, merely a map, or metaphor, and does not necessarily describe the territory, or reality. The questions that are allowed, and thus the answers we obtain, are controlled by what our theory frames for us to describe. Indeed,

> Problems that remain insoluble should always be suspected as questions asked in the wrong way, like the problems of cause and effect. Make a spurious division of one process into two, forget that you have done it, and then puzzle for centuries as to how to get the two together.(Watts, 1966, p. 53)

Systems theory is a unifying theory. Instead of studying objects and people discretely, we now have a means of studying them in relationship. Along with the other systems we have invented, e.g., the solar system,

5

society, culture, neighborhoods, bureaucracy, we have also found it quite useful to construe the family as a system.

The systems perspective would have us see each member of a family in relation to other family members, as each affects and is affected by the other persons. According to systems theory, it makes no sense to analyze any person independently. To understand each person in a family, one must study how each is in relation to every other family member. To study one apart from the others, out of the context of the family relationships, is to know that person relative to the new context (the context in which he or she is studied) but not in the context of his or her family relationships.

If a person is studied in isolation, then the inquiry must be concerned with the nature of the human mind. If the field of inquiry is expanded to include the interaction of behaviors and the context in which it occurs, the focus shifts from the isolated monad, which does not exist within systems theory, to the relationships between the parts of a system. The observer of human behavior then turns from an inferential study of the mind to the observable manifestations of relationship.

Since the components of a human system are interrelated, it follows that each family member's behavior cannot be viewed and treated as an isolated unit. Rather, it must be considered relative to context, as both antecedent and subsequent to the behavior of other family members. Thus all events in a family are simultaneously subsequent and antecedent behaviors.

To be consistent with the systems perspective, we must use the same framework to view families in general. The family as a system is a component, or subsystem, of a larger network of systems, the suprasystem. Therefore, to understand each family, one must study how that family is in relationship with other families in their broader societal and cultural contexts. As individuals within a family interface and interact with one another, so families interface and interact with other family systems and other systems. Just as an individual is studied in the context of his or her family, so the family is studied in the context of its environment.

The systems perspective therefore moves us away from linear cause-effect thinking, i.e., that A influences B but B does not influence A:

"I treat you like a child because you behave like a child."

"I behave like a child because you treat me like a child."

A ⟶ B

6

The systems perspective moves us to a reciprocal or circular notion of causality, i.e., A and B are in dynamic interaction:

> "When I treat you like a child, you behave like a child, and then I treat you like a child even more and you behave even more like a child. We sure have a vicious cycle going, don't we."

> "When I behave like a child, you treat me like a child, and then I behave like a child even more and you treat me like a child even more. We are sure caught up with each other, aren't we."

With a systems perspective, therefore, our view of "reality" would have us perceive with Bronowski (1978) a "constantly conjoined universe" in which ultimate knowledge, or truth, is not accessible to us. The theoretical relativity which is a part of this framework would describe good and bad in all frameworks but no one absolute good. The notions of interdependence and relationship entail our understanding individuals and families in mutual interaction and in the context of their environments. Causality becomes a reciprocal concept to be found in the interface between individuals and between systems. Responsibility exists only as a bilateral process. In the following chapter we shall attempt to further delineate the concepts which characterize a systems perspective.

Chapter 3

DEFINITIONS OF SYSTEMS CONCEPTS

> General System Theory is the skeleton
> of science in the sense that it aims to
> provide a framework or structure of
> systems on which to hang the flesh and
> blood of particular disciplines and
> particular subject matters in an orderly
> and coherent corpus of knowledge.
>
> Kenneth Boulding

Like all theories, systems theory has concepts and constructs which have meanings specific to the theory. From a systems perspective, you will find neither intrapsychic labels, such as ego, self-concept, drive, self-aware-ness, etc., nor labels assigning internal motivation, such as the concepts of discounting, selfish, rescuing, etc., as descriptors of behavior. Similarly, the concepts of influence, control, purpose and goal are meaningless in the context of a systems framework. What you do find are labels which describe interpersonal processes, or the observable dynamics which occur when elements of a system interface and when systems (as elements of a larger, supra-system) interface with other systems.

Several key constructs are defined in this chapter. However, it should be remembered that each phenomenon under study tends to interact with the theory that seeks to explain that phenomenon. So it is when we use a systems perspective to study the family. It is not that the theory is necessarily corrupted, but rather that we, as creative human beings, define according to our personal frames of reference the constructs and concepts which we use to describe that which we study. Thus the differences we observe are those we have created by the theory or map we employ in an attempt to understand or explore our world.

The definitions and explanations provided in this book are interpretations which we find useful in the study of families, and as we work to help families through therapy or development and enrichment activities. If our explanations differ from the "party line," it is because we assume the same right to create as did the seminal theorists on whose work we build. Where our explanations differ, we do not deprecate in any way the efforts of others; we merely reserve the right to describe our own interpretation-- our own systems perspective. We find it helpful. Perhaps you will find it helpful as well.

The concepts we have chosen for inclusion in this chapter are the following:

Boundaries

Communication/Information Processing

Entropy and Negative Entropy

Equifinality

Homeostasis, Morphostasis and Morphogenesis

Open and Closed Systems

Positive and Negative Feedback

Purpose or Goal

Relationship

Wholeness

Boundaries

A fundamental characteristic of systems is that they have boundaries. In the family system, this boundary is defined by the redundant patterns of behavior which characterize the relationships within that system and by those values which are sufficiently distinct as to give a family its particular identity. Family members are defined, and are thus able to be distinguished from other families and systems, by the information or communication which flows between them.

Most people are members of several different systems. To some extent, each relationship within a particular system defines and is defined by the relationships in all the other systems of which one is a member. The amount of information permitted into a system from without, or the rigidity of the

10

boundary, is indicative of the openness or closedness of a system.

If a family or other system accepts too much information from without, the boundaries of that system become indistinct and are not discernable as separate from other systems. On the other hand, if the boundaries are too rigid, the system will not be sufficiently flexible to effectively process information from its environment. The system must constantly interact with the environment in which it exists and boundaries enable that system to both accept useful information and screen out information deemed unacceptable.

The concept of boundary implies a hierarchy of systems. A family system is but one "defined" system which is described as existing as a part of a larger system, or suprasystem. By defining the concept of boundaries, we connote the separateness of a system from a larger system and yet a belongingness to that suprasystem. Similarly, a family is a system and is also a part of the system of all families. And subsystems of relationships exist within the larger system of the family.

Maintenance of family identity involves a process in which the boundary functions as a buffer for information from outside the system, screening it for compatibility with the family value system. Thus when a family member also considers becoming a part of another system, that system will be examined with an eye for discerning behavior patterns and values which are reasonably compatible with those of the family system.

The boundary also describes the "exit" for information from the system. Such information is different from the inputs of other systems and is not purely what happened within the system. Rather, incoming information is transformed by the system and is then emitted as new information to other systems.

In summary, we define the boundary as that region through which inputs and outputs must pass, during which exchanges with the systems in an environment reflect the interactive process (Berrien, 1968). Thus a boundary describes the possibility of energy or information transfer, in either direction, between all systems which interface in reasonable proximity to one another.

Communication/Information Processing

Communication patterns define the nature of the relationship in a family system. Three modes of communication have been identified:

11

1. Verbal or Digital

2. Non-Verbal }
3. Context   } Analog

Verbal communication refers to the words or labels we use to transmit information. Also known as the report or digital mode, verbal communication is considered the least powerful element in defining the nature of a relationship or system: "Indeed, whenever relationship is the central issue of communication, we find that digital (verbal) language is almost meaningless" (Watzlawick, Beavin & Jackson, 1967, p. 63). For example, the explicit content of the sentence, "The garbage is piling up," is purely descriptive. Without specifying other aspects of the relationship between speaker and listener, the probable response is non-specific.

Non-verbal communication refers to such things as voice tone, gestures, facial expression, body posture, inflection, etc. Non-verbal behavior is the command, or relationship-defining mode of communication. In effect, it tells the receiver of a message what to do with the message. The non-verbal mode is the part of the message that comments upon how the message is to be handled, or the nature of the sender's meaning. It refers to the sender's intention. Thus the sentence, "The garbage is piling up," stated by a father to a son in the kitchen probably contains the indirect command, "Take the garbage out." Every non-verbal communication can be verbalized or made digital.

Context is closely associated with non-verbal communication, and together these two modes comprise the analog. Typically a change in context will elicit a change in the rules of a relationship. Where we are, with whom, and when defines how we relate, for example, when we are with friends, at home, in church, etc. The context is capable of making the non-verbal verbal and it also subsumes or qualifies the non-verbal mode. The non-verbal, in turn, qualifies the verbal mode of communication:

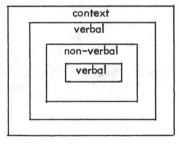

The statement, "The garbage is piling up," made by father to son in the context of the kitchen probably comminicated the command, "Take the garbage out". However, the same verbal message spoken by father to son in the city landfill would have an entirely different meaning.

As a relationship (system) develops, its members consciously or unconsciously become sensitized to analog, to the definitions of their mutual interaction. Each person acts in a manner consistent with the nature of the relationship desired. The desired pattern of interaction may be defined by each person's belief system, which evolved in his or her family of origin. Thus reciprocal analogical signals are exchanged and tend to define the nature of the relationship.

Information flow is the basic process of a social system. Social systems are held together and change by the transfer of information/energy within and between the boundaries of different systems. Information/energy exchange implies a capacity for action and the ability to move toward either stability or change. However, to be useful, information/energy derived from both the characteristics and resources of members and from other systems must be organized; it must be neither random nor noise. With a high level of organized information flow, a system will move toward greater complexity, organization and an increased capacity to survive. That is, it will increase in negative entropy. Low level and disorganized information flow indicates movement toward entropy, a disorganized state characterized by a gradual but decreasing level of interaction between members.

In general, the lower the rate of the information flow, the more static and predictable, or entropic, a system becomes. On the other hand, a dynamic system is increasingly more unpredictable and marked by change as energy and power are shifted within. For human systems, this energy is the information flow, organized at higher and higher frequencies to enable the system to stabilize and/or adapt to change as necessary, and thus to continue its existence and maintain a state of negative entropy.

Several principles of communication relate to the understanding of information processing within a family:

Principle One. One cannot not behave. We do not have the choice of doing nothing so long as we live. Statements like, "I'm not doing anything," or, "I'm doing nothing," deny their own message and affirm the principle.

Principle Two. One cannot not communicate. All behavior in the context of others has message value. Indeed, even silence is a form of communication. Whether you intend to communicate or not, there is message

13

value in every behavior or combination of behaviors you do. Thus, the statement, "We just don't communicate," describes perhaps dissatisfaction with how the speaker feels about the relationship, but there is communication. We have a choice to communicate verbally, but we have no choice except to communicate analogically. Those who observe you will interpret meaning relative to your behavior and your relationship to them.

Principle Three. The meaning of a given behavior is not the "true" meaning of the behavior; it is, however, that individual's personal truth. Any number of interpretations can be given to any set of behaviors. The way in which we define a behavior is thus associated with our previous experiences in similar situations and we make a fit between our beliefs, observations, and the events we experience. For many people, the meaning they experience constitutes for them the only meaning of an event rather than one among many possible meanings. Whatever meaning a person experiences in a given situation, it is probable that more credence is given to analogical messages than to verbal messages.

Entropy and Negative Entropy

All living systems are open to some degree. Although the degree of openness may vary, a living system has some exchange with other systems in its environment. A family system accepts from other systems only inputs that are necessary for its continued existence. Entropy refers to the lack of energy or information in a system. Negative entropy (negentropy) describes the tendency away from maximum disorder. Input of new energy, which takes the form of information or communication between a system and other systems in its environment, is the basis of the negentropic trend in human systems like the family. While no family system is closed, in those more nearly closed, there is little new energy or information. In an open system, entropy may increase, remain the same, or decrease. All living systems are open and thus are capable of, "intake of matter rich in high energy, maintenance of a high degree of order and even advancement..." (Bertalanffy, 1968, p. 159).

A family is constantly bombarded with input (energy/information) from other systems. In the process of retaining its identity as distinct from other systems, it interacts with this energy input, processes it, and emits outputs to other systems which carry the family's distinctive mark. These outputs are energy transfers from the family to other systems, which may regard them as useful or useless (waste), i.e., not useful energy.

All systems need useful energy inputs to increase negative entropy. Without useful inputs, systems tend toward maximum disorder, or entropy.

14

In such a state, the lack of structure or excess uncertainty may be defined as noise, or error.

A portion of the energy of a system is used to organize the system. Some energy is directed toward task functions. Too much energy directed toward maintenance functions at the expense of task functions can be problematic. Families can spend hours hassling over how to organize,   how to organize to get organized, etc. Similarly, the family can go about the task of fami-ly life in a seemingly random and often conflictual manner, as little or no energy is directed toward maintenance functions. In a disorganized system the members lack a coherent sense of relationship and energy is expended thoughtlessly or in a random manner. The movement of the system at this point is toward entropy.

Equifinality

According to this construct, no matter where one begins, the end will be the same. Put another way, there are many different means to the same end, for equifinality is, "The tendency towards a characteristic final state from different initial states and in different ways based upon dynamic interaction in an open system attaining a steady state" (Bertalanffy, 1968, p. 46).

The concept of equifinality precludes the need for an historical perspec-tive, which some other psychological theories view as essential for success-ful counseling. Thus, with systems theory, the important question for the therapist becomes "what" rather than "why." The focus is on the here and now rather than on past history or the need for insight. The origins of a particular family situation are not considered to be nearly as important in therapy as is the organization of the ongoing interaction in that family.

The key is the pattern, and equifinality would have us observe the ex-isting redundant patterns of which the communication or feedback processes in a given system are comprised. For in many cases, it is the attempted solutions, or the repetition of dysfunctional patterns which maintain a so-called "problem," which are in fact problematic.

The patterns of communication serve the function of maintaining the system in a steady-state around a problem. However, since an absolute steady-state in a system is probably not possible, pathology tends to increase as a near steady-state becomes a part of the redundant pattern of communi-cation.

Given the idea of equifinality, what you see is what you get, and that is all you need to know. Or, "The system is its own best explanation and the study of its present organization the appropriate methodology" (Watzla-wick, Beavin & Jackson, 1967, p. 129). In other words, the way a family is interacting in the present provides the therapist with sufficient information to intervene effectively. Activating change mechanisms within the system involves a focus on the family processes as well as interaction with the here and now communication and feedback and thus with the structure and organization of the family.

Homeostasis, Morphostasis and Morphogenesis

Homeostasis is the construct which describes a system's tendency toward stability, or steady-state. Maintained by negative feedback, this state of dynamic equilibrium, or homeostatic balance, refers to the system's capacity to be stable.

Although useful, the concept of homeostasis is somewhat restrictive and misleading. A system seeks stability. Yet to continue to be healthy, it must also be able to change. Thus, the two related concepts of morphostasis and morphogenesis (Speer, 1970) were developed to augment the steady-state dynamic defined by homeostasis.

As described by Speer, morphostasis is similar in meaning to homeostasis. Morphogenesis, however, delineates the system-enhancing behavior that allows for growth, creativity, innovation and change, which are all characteristic of functional families.

In a healthy family system, morphogenesis (change) and morphostasis (stability) are both necessary. Thus there is a tendency in a relationship or a system to offset differences exhibited by one of the members. While either extreme of the morphogenesis-morphostasis continuum would probably be dysfunctional, in healthy families, a balance will be maintained between the two. That is, the rules of the system will allow for change in the rules governing the system.

In times of stress, morphogenesis is probably desirable. However, were change permitted too frequently or to too great a degree, the stability of the family would be threatened. (This is discussed further under Open and Closed Systems).

The ability to change is also necessary as the family and its members grow and develop. A child is not always five years old, and if the patterns of parenting do not change as the child grows in order to meet the demands of each developmental stage, the parent-child system becomes dysfunctional. Similarly, parenting a five year old with behavior appropriate for an older child is dysfunctional. Indeed, "The art of progress is to preserve order amid change and preserve change amid order" (Alfred North Whitehead).

Open and Closed Systems—

The particular behavior patterns of the relationships within a system define that system. When the system is healthy, it will evolve as the characteristics of its members and their relationships change. Such changes do not disrupt the essential continuity of the system, and its continued existence is therefore assured.

Openness and closedness refer to the boundaries a family establishes among family members and between itself and other systems. The more input family members allow from other family members, or a family allows from other systems, the more it is an open system. Conversely, the less input, the more closed. As with morphogenesis and morphostasis, in the functional family, a healthy balance between the two extremes seems most desirable.

Input from within a family and from other systems represents pressure to change. If not enough change is allowed to occur, a system is said to be closed, although, as we have noted, all living systems are open to some degree. If too much change is permitted, that system is said to be open to a fault. A system can be dysfunctional by being either too open or too closed. In the former case it loses its identity as a system distinct from other systems, and in the latter case, it exists totally outside the sphere of other systems.

In a healthy system, neither openness nor closedness is good per se. For example, in a hostile environment, maintaining a closed system may be the only way to assure continuation of that system. In general, however, if a system changes either too fast or not enough, it can be problematic. Thus, ideally, the governing rules of a system should allow for accommodation to gradual developmental growth pressures.

The ideal pace of change in a system is probably idiosyncratic to that system, as tempered by input from outside, which is in turn a response to output from the system. Further, it is unlikely that all members of a family system will value the same rate of change.

Adolescents, reflecting the ever increasing input from other systems, may want more rapid change in the family system than that desired by their parents. Thus the parents of adolescents often act to modify or restrict the nature of the rate of change. Similarly, a woman who tries to alter the marital relationship in response to values derived from the women's liberation viewpoint may find her husband closed to this new information. Yet, if the system is to be functional, change needs to be accommodated by the system in some way, to some degree. The contract between parent and child that was effective when the child was younger will not be functional for the adolescent-parent relationship. And the marital relationship that existed prior to the wife's exposure to the feminist point of view will need to change in some way or the marriage may end.

Positive and Negative Feedback

Communication, or information flow, is the energy input and output of human systems. This communication can also be described as feedback about whether the product of a system is useful or not (waste). The usual form of feedback within and between human systems is in one of the communication modes described earlier, i.e., verbal, non-verbal and context, or verbal and analog. Stated somewhat differently, they describe what was communicated, how, and where.

Feedback is responsive to forces which are disturbing to the system. Thus, if persons A and B have established a fairly stable relationship pattern, and if A behaves in a manner exceeding the acceptable limits of the relationship, (which is probably feedback that the existing contract is not satisfactory or that B's behavior exceeds acceptable limits), B may give feedback to A in an attempt to return to the steady-state of the previous relationship contract. In this way mutual interaction and feedback occur in an ongoing pattern of reciprocal interaction.

In classical general systems terminology, negative feedback is a message that the output by another has reached some predetermined maximum level and is an indication to cut off or reduce the inputs. Positive feedback is the reverse situation and means that the output is less than some maximum, and the feedback loop signals to allow more inputs (Berrien, 1968).

As defined above, feedback seeks to maintain near steady-state functioning, tempering external variation that would otherwise cause fluctuation. Feedback therefore serves to increase the probability of the survival of the system.

As one cannot not communicate, one cannot not give feedback analogically. Thus, in human systems, communication can be equated with feedback. Family members will want other family members to behave according to the feedback they give each other. And feedback about behavior will be consistent with what one believes; it must be self-validating. We communicate, or give feedback consistent with our ways of thinking and believing. We interact with others according to our models of how we think they should be.

18

In a family, a certain degree of stability is necessary, and feedback serves to promote the desired stability. Yet, in a family, feedback processes are also useful in promoting change in response to changes in family members or circumstances. The feedback processes seek to promote increases and decreases in behavior valued by the family system within a tolerable range of variation.

A family's feedback mechanisms may seek an increase in outputs of ten year old behavior from a ten year old child, and a decrease in outputs of five year old behavior from the same child. Similarly, a family's feedback mechanisms may seek to reduce outputs of fifteen year old behavior in a fifteen year old, and may try to increase outputs of behavior appropriate for a twelve year old. In the latter case, the feedback process may be dysfunctional.

In popular usage, the label, "positive feedback," generally refers to praise, or a similar behavior, i.e., positive reinforcement. Negative feedback usually refers to criticism or some form of harassment, i.e., positive or negative punishment. As applied to families from a systems perspective, positive and negative feedback are defined quite differently, and each may take the form of either criticism or praise. Whether or not feedback is positive or negative is relative to the context of the system.

Positive feedback in systems terms is a message that change has taken place. It is a recognition that such change has been accommodated by the system or family. Positive feedback is therefore a deviation-amplifying mechanism which indicates that system maintenance behavior has occurred in response to change. For example, grounding a child as a means of punishment for some unacceptable behavior is positive feedback.

Negative feedback maintains the status quo and thus performs a homeostatic, or morphostatic function. For example, praise is a form of negative feedback when it tends to elicit repetition of the behavior that preceded it. If a behavior beyond the range of a family's tolerance occurs and is acknowledged by either praise or criticism, this initial response is positive feedback. From that point on, however, whether the behavior is praise or criticism, it is negative feedback, or a response that maintains the status quo.

Many parents believe that criticism is an effective mechanism for behavior change. However, criticism (positive feedback) in response to a new behavior that is beyond acceptable limits may serve a deviation-amplifying function. Thus, the initial response to new behavior is important in families. Instead of a critical response to a new, undesirable behavior, a more useful response is feedforward, or a redirection of the behavior to fit family values.

19

To a fifteen year old who stayed out too late, this might take the following form: "We expect you to be home on time. We know how hard it is to tell your friends that you need to call your parents, but this is what we expect of you when you cannot return at the appointed time."

Feedforward is thus a request for a behavior that is desired but has not yet occurred: "Would you hold me?" instead of "You never hold me." Feedforward as an alternative to criticism can avoid reciprocal criticism, which is the logical response. That is, criticism begets criticism. However, it is foolish to criticize someone for criticizing someone.

The occurrence of a new behavior in a family suggests that change may be necessary in order for the family to be stable in a functional way. To the fifteen year old mentioned above, it is a natural process to want to move toward more separation and to have more frequent contact with persons outside the family system. This does and will occur. Therefore, how a family defines this occurrence is the key, not whether it will or will not happen. And a response of punishment preceded by arguing and an exchange of heated words can make the peer group more attractive, and may serve to build this response pattern into the family.

Negative feedback as a homeostatic mechanism can, through praise of a twelve year old, maintain a context that defines expectations on the part of all concerned so that twelve year old behavior in an individual continues well into adulthood. Similarly, the initial harassment and punitive response (positive feedback) to staying out too late, as well as the accompanying arguments, tend to remain in the system with increasing frequency and greater intensity. Thus negative feedback not only maintains the status quo, it also amplifies existing patterns in a family.

Haley (1963) suggested that family problems generally emerge when a family needs to move to the next developmental stage and gets hung up. The appropriate use of feedback mechanisms coupled with an understanding of developmental stages of individuals and families may therefore go a long way towards preventing problems from arising.

Purpose or Goal

Systems are described as purposive, or goal oriented. The organization or structure, the network of relationships, and the nature of the relationships within a system are relative to the purpose of the system. The interrelationships of parts qualify the joint behavior of members of a system in accordance with the purpose of a system.

However, specifying the purpose or goal of a system is problematic without making recourse to intrapsychic processes such as needs or desires of individual members. This activity is not legitimate in systems theory. And to state that the purpose or goal of a system is to maintain itself begs the question of the assumption of purpose or goal of a system.

Goals and purposes of systems, therefore, tend to be inferential and definitional like systems themselves. Perhaps that which we call "heaps" or "aggregates" are not systems because, and only because, we have not observed a regularity or interrelationship of parts and a purpose or goal behind the interrelations which might exist but have not been observed. In a sense, it is like calling a weed a weed only because we have not found a practical use for the plant we call a weed.

Observing regularities does not mean that the regularities exist per se. Yet, we observe redundant patterns of familial interaction and it becomes useful to define the family as a system. It is also useful for us to describe distinctions between plants and animals. However, given another model, such a distinction may not be useful, and we may find it more meaningful to describe the distinction between living and non-living phenomena.

We are accustomed to thinking of a family as having a mother, father, and children. However, we are now being confronted with alternative family forms: single parent, restructured, kibbutz, commune, to name but a few. These are probably construed as family systems, although to many they may be "weeds."

To say that a system's purpose is to receive inputs, process these inputs, and produce outputs to other systems is another possibility. Indeed, this is what it does. However, in terms of goal or purpose, this too is problematic in its circularity. Therefore, we will probably need to look to ourselves as observers who choose and find it useful to define families, schools, communities, etc., as systems. What usefulness is there in so defining these phenomena? What do we learn when we observe, or do we, in our need to understand our world, see regularities where in fact there may be none? Inasmuch as we cannot transcend ourselves, our theories, definitions, and perceived regularities are our own inventions.

Relationship

This construct describes the patterns of interaction between two or more individuals. It also describes the rules governing how one family member is with another or how they relate to each other. The energy transmitted in a relationship takes the form of information exchange or communication, both

21

verbal and analogical, between the participants.

When two people meet, they immediately exchange behaviors which define the nature of their relationship. In the initial, as well as in each subsequent contact, the behavior of each interacts with the behavior of the other as both continue to define their relationship. Thus a relationship may be seen as a bargain or contract about how and under what circumstances each will exchange certain kinds of behavior with the other. And as the interaction proceeds, each message exchange limits the number of possibilities for acceptable behaviors in that relationship (Watzlawick, Beavin & Jackson, 1967).

After a number of exchanges have taken place, a stable, redundant pattern of behavior emerges. It can then be predicted that each person will be a certain way with the other. Predictability, which is the logical product of redundancy, generates trust: "I know who you are and who I am with you; the way you are with me, the way I am with you."

It is the redundant patterns of interaction between and among family members which distinguish their system of relationships from any other system. These patterns may be called rules, and they usually exist outside the awareness of the people in a relationship.

We may infer the rules of a relationship based on our observation of the regularities in these redundant patterns of interaction. Such implicit rules are the keys both to our understanding and to the definition of a particular relationship. And although the participants may have certain explicit rules for their relationship, these are of secondary importance to its definition.

The concept of relationship, therefore, refers to that which we infer when we observe members of a system exchanging redundant patterns of behavior. Relationship thus denotes the interdependence described under Wholeness: It is the third part of the equation $1 + 1 = 3$.

The appropriate units of analysis in the study of human systems are the relationships between members and the organization or rules for these relationships. From intrapsychic psychology we have a rich vocabulary to describe individuals. For example, we have labels such as introverted, extroverted, dominant, submissive, kind, cruel, etc. However, in the relatively new application of systems theory to human behavior, we do not have the same richness of categories to describe the relationship patterns we observe. One of the few that has been described is symbiosis, which refers to the dependance for continuation of a particular behavior in one person upon the continuation of a particular behavior in another. Accordingly, the behav -

iors mutually feed and maintain each other.

Bateson (1972) provided an assist in the development of a relationship
labeling system when he observed patterns in native tribes during anthropo-
logical field studies. He termed these relationships complementary and symmetrical. Watzlawick, Beavin and Jackson (1967) refined these concepts,
which are defined as follows: A complementary relationship is one in which
the interaction between two people is characterized by a high frequency of
exchanges of opposite kinds of behavior. A symmetrical relationship is one
in which the interaction between two people is characterized by a high frequency of the same kinds of behavior.

One may usually identify these relationship styles by observing the exchanges of analogic behavior. For example, in a relationship labeled complementary, one might observe what is often described as a one-up, one-
down exchange:

Person One	Person Two
Leans forward............................	Leans back
Commands................................	Acquiesces
Head erect..............................	Head down
Loud voice.............................	Soft voice
Do this !...............................	Yes, dear.

The typical explanation for exchanges like the above is that one person
is in a dominant position and the other is in a powerless or submissive position. However, this generally accepted interpretation is not consistent with
the systems framework. Rather, from a systems perspective, each person in a
relationship is equally powerful, and the old meaning of "control" no longer
applies. Thus one could characterize a complementary relationship as one
in which the members are using opposite behaviors in an attempt to narrow
down the number of possible next moves by the other. And complementary
behavior can therefore be construed as unilateral efforts to regulate a relationship, efforts which must fail, since a relationship, by definition, is bilateral (Palazzoli, Boscolo, Cecchin & Prata, 1978).

Dominance which seems to "cause" (linear) submission may look like
"control" at one level. However, reciprocally, submission which seems to
effect a momentary stoppage of dominant behavior can be construed as an
attempt to change that behavior. According to Bateson (Brand, 1974), in a
relationship the illusion of the possibility of unilateral control is often the
problem.

23

In a relationship labeled symmetrical, one might observe escalating exchanges of the same kinds of behavior. Examples of exchanges characterizing symmetrical relationships are as follows:

Person One	Person Two
Commands........................	Commands
Shouts	Shouts
Scowls	Scowls
Attacks.........................	Attacks

Complementary and symmetrical exchanges are good or bad relative to context. Both seem to be a part of every relationship, including those labeled functional. But in functional relationships there seems to be something more. Thus a third relationship style, parallel, was defined by Lederer and Jackson (1967), and later refined by Scoresby and Christensen (1976). Research by Harper, Scoresby and Boyce (1977) suggested that the parallel relationship style is of a higher logical order than are complementary or symmetrical relationships, which are comprised of behaviors either logically the same or logically the opposite.

A parallel relationship is one in which each person alternates in the complementary, or one-up, one-down, positions and includes a combination of symmetrical and complementary behaviors. Further, both members accept responsibility for things that go wrong between them. There is a high level and high quality of information exchange with approximately the same ratio of listening and expression for each member. Decisions are made by agreement, with a sharing of information and consideration of the ideas of both.

Parallel relationships are characterized particularly by greater variation of behaviors, and are not limited to exchanges of the same (symmetrical) or opposite (complementary) behaviors although these are a part of the relationship. Parallel relationships seem divested of the power struggle, with each member willing to reciprocally take the one-down position based on the merits of the ideas of the other. A greater frequency of logically different behavior, i.e., different from more of the same or opposite behaviors, is observed. People in parallel relationships seem to recognize the inherent bilateral nature of relationships.

Wholeness

In a system the whole is greater than the sum of the parts, or $1 + 1 = 3$. Two people relating together are not independent. Rather, they mutually interact with one another. It is their interaction which adds the third element to the above equation.

In any relationship, the people involved are mutually responsive to one another. When looking at a family, one must see the organismic whole as well as the way one individual acts in relation to another. One must look at the organization of the system, or the structure which results from the interaction of the members of that system. One must understand that only when studied in the context of the whole can the behavior of an individual be fully understood.

As the number of members of a system increases, the complexity of the system also increases. A dyad is comprised of the two persons plus the relationship between them, or three units. A family of five has five persons plus ten relationships, or fifteen units. Further, each relationship in a system affects every other person and every other relationship to a greater or lesser degree. For as Bowen (Guerin, 1976, p. 76) has noted, the triangle may well be, "The smallest stable relationship system." Thus while a dyad may be relatively stable during calm times, as soon as difficulties arise, a third person is often drawn in to form a triangle, or a two against one situation, in order to solve a problem. Indeed, the concept of wholeness moves our family of five persons into a very complex system comprised of five persons, ten relationships and twenty-seven triangles, for a total of forty-two units!

To summarize, wholes must be understood as being different from the sum of their parts. Further, because of the interrelatedness of components, a change in one part will have an impact on the whole. Rather than being independent elements, communication exchanges are inseparable. The total system has a unique coherence and may thus be said to be non-summative. For adding the parts will not produce the whole and members are not independent of one another as in the case with summativity.

That which we choose to call a "heap", the phenomenon in which we do not observe interrelatedness, would be summativity. Change in one element would occur in isolation from other elements since the parts are not connected and thus do not have the property of wholeness. However, as one begins to think and observe from a systems perspective, one can no longer discern such unrelated phenomena. For as one thinks in terms of an interrelatedness of all elements in all systems, the possibility that a "heap" exists is reduced to zero, except for instructional purposes. If summativity in any phenomenon is not observed, the property of non-summativity becomes the only property possible and thus self-destructs since its opposite identity member, summativity, has no meaning.

The above discussion illustrates the recurring dilemma which we have encountered as we have attempted to define key concepts within the systems framework. We used the construct summative-non-summative to explain the concept of wholeness. However, as our discussion progressed it became apparent that while useful in one sense, the summative-non-summative construct does not fit the constantly conjoined universe in which all elements are interrelated which systems theory suggests.

What we have done is to use a construct from one theory (one in which independent elements are possible) to explain another theory (one in which all elements are interrelated). We recognize the dilemma and it only reinforces our awareness of the inadequacies of our language system in explaining interrelated phenomena. We therefore reach into other theories for concepts which may be useful in bridging the gap and yet we realize that this device used for teaching purposes is not entirely satisfactory. We need a richer language for describing relational concepts and yet this language must "make sense," or be able to bridge other models and thus facilitate a change in epistemology.

Chapter 4

FAMILY INTERPRETIVE SYSTEMS

> What we perceive or overlook in the
> field of our potential experience de-
> pends on the framework or concepts
> we have in our minds.
>
> Icheiser

As you read this book, you are learning about a model of the world, a
story, a map of the reality we assume exists but cannot know. Systems theory, like other theories is only one explanation. Systems theory, like other
theories, is an invention of people: "Again, man cannot transcend himself
..., so that no matter what modes of perception or what sorts of world interpretation he chooses, they are still his own" (Seidler, 1979, p. 52).

We as social scientists often view what we do as unique to us. We seek
valid explanations which we can use to understand, predict and control our
world. Kelly (1955) made a useful contribution when he described people
in general, as well as scientists, as being engaged in the same enterprise.
For he described all people as scientists who observe, form hypotheses, con-
duct experiments to test the validity of their predictions relative to their interpretive systems. This process takes a circular course according to the
frame of reference, or interpretive system, we "scientists" use. Thus we are
free to see the world and interpret its events in a manner consistent with our
frame of reference, but we are constrained by our particular perspective
from definitions which might be possible in the context of another framework.

The truth or falseness of an interpretive system is not discernable. However, the degree of usefulness of a theory is personally decidable relative
to context. For us as scholars and scientists we probably will choose to use

the frame that seems better than its rivals; that is, when it can explain and predict the facts and solve the problems of interest to us.

Both individual members of families and family units have interpretive systems. Spouses in a family system bring to their new family the elements of the interpretive systems they learned in their families of origin. This merger of frames in the married couple is characterized by a process of blending the two frames. Indeed, it has been suggested that people are, at least in part, attracted to each other on the basis of the compatibility of their interpretive systems.

To the degree that there is agreement or disagreement of frames of reference, we could assume a compatibility or lack of harmony plus pressure on one another to adapt and/or modify their behavior and thus their frames. However, according to Kuhn (1970), an interpretive system can never be entirely adequate. There are some things it cannot explain or predict and there will always be at least one "violation of paradigm expectation." Such variations are called anomalies.

Anomalies are initially unnoticed. An interpretive system implicitly defines and imposes boundaries which prevent the early recognition of anomalies, which are thus unimportant or irrelevant at the outset. Sooner or later, however, these anomalies are recognized for what they are, e.g., genuine problems for the paradigm, or interpretive system. Attempts may be made to assimilate an anomaly within the interpretive frame or to adapt the theory to account for the anomaly, thereby eliminating the apparent conflict. For if an anomaly cannot be assimilated by a theory, the model itself is threatened. Indeed, the inability of an existing theory to handle such an anomaly usually signals the beginning of a search for a new theory (Kuhn, 1970).

If the anomalous phenomenon is sufficiently deviant, scientists may turn their attention from existing research to an investigation of and explanation for this phenomenon. Such efforts may involve a questioning of the adequacy of the standard paradigm and may result in the formulation of a new paradigm or theory in which the phenomenon fits and is thus no longer an anomaly. And so the process of scientific "revolutions" repeats itself.

Kuhn's model of scientific revolutions is a useful metaphor to explain the "progress of science" within families. As stated previously, one could describe the initial formation of a new family, at least in part, as an apparent compatibility and merging of interpretive frames. An interpretive frame can be thought of as containing within it a set of constructs of paired opposites which provide the basis for experiencing meaning for events that occur in the perceptual field. A few of the constructs which may exist within such an interpretive frame are as follows:

Category	Opposite Category
Good	Bad
Cooperative	Competitive
Easy	Hard
Strong	Weak
Support	Neglect
Happy	Sad
Passive	Active

A given stimulus event may activate certain of these paired opposites in order to provide a meaning for the experience. For example, the stimulus event "religion" may activate any of the following:

RELIGION

Category	Opposite Category
Good	Bad
Strong	Weak
Support	Neglect
Happy	Sad

The constructs in the interpretive system provide direct links to experienced meaning, feelings, and action. The bi-polar nature of the constructs parallels a positive or negative affective response. People would therefore describe a religious experience according to their interpretive systems and behave in a manner that is logical to it. This process can be illustrated as follows:

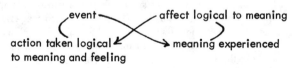

Each newly married couple will experience anomalies in the behavior of the other which do not fit the interpretive system brought with them from their families of origin. These frames of reference were familized into them in their years of experience within their families. Each individual may seek to impose his/her set of constructs on the marital relationship. Daily contact provides a number of issues and experiences for the discovery of anomalies in the behavior of the other in such areas as sex, degree of separateness,

29

acceptable, nurturance, money management, parenting practices, etc. Successful marriages and families develop a new interpretive system unique to the new family. They retain commonly shared constructs from their families of origin, but evolve new interpretive systems when anomalies are experienced.

A couple may be aware of certain explicit rules brought from the interpretive systems of their families of origin. However, the rules that are the most important are probably implicit. Such rules are tied to corresponding interpretive systems and may not be consciously experienced. Rather, they are generally activated automatically. These are the implicit "shoulds," or the "way it is supposed to be," for each role in the family, e.g., husband, wife, mother, father, breadwinner, keeper of the castle.

A family's interpretive system may also be inferred from the metaphors it uses to describe itself and its members. The types and kinds of labels assigned reveal how a family defines reality and the categories which comprise its interpretive system. Such metaphors are basic to the understanding of each family's story.

A couple may experience a minimum of difficulty in adjusting and forming a new family if their interpretive systems are flexible rather than rigid. An interpretive system with the meta-perspective that there is more than one interpretation can transcend any specific explanation and look for alternatives when anomalies are encountered around specific issues. This is important for the initial adjustment to marriage as well as for dealing with subsequent developmental crises which occur throughout the family life cycle.

Within a family, the rules, values, and beliefs in the interpretive system must be flexible if the family is to contribute to the normal development of its members. There needs to be both stability and change. A couple may change its ideas about marriage and families from what they anticipated to what is actually experienced. And the interpretive system necessary while children are young must change when children become adolescents if the family is to continue to be happy and to foster normal development. Family problems may lie in the failure of the family to make necessary transitions to different stages during the course of the development of its members. A functional interpretive system is subscribed to with a certain tentativeness and is sufficiently flexible to allow for movement to successive stages of growth and development.

It is our position that a family's interpretive system is most useful to its members when it is based on a systems perspective, i.e., a frame that sees the interdependence of the members of a family system. Further, we believe that the functional interpretive system would contain knowledge of normal developmental stages of individuals and families and would thus allow for a smooth transition from one stage to another. It is also useful, as mentioned above, for the interpretive system to contain a meta-perspective which allows for the possibility of alternative explanations or new metaphors, and contains rules for changing the rules about the family and family life as the need arises. This system is open and yet closed, and can help family members acquire what seems to be a necessary balance between the seemingly contradictory but essential ingredients of a satisfying relationship. The family provides a context that defines stability relative to its ability to change.

In any relationship there will be "violoations of the paradigm," or anomalies which are anomalies only from a specific interpretive system. With relativistic thinking, there is a greater probability that these anomalies can be given a constructive definition rather than that they will contribute to the deterioration of the relationship. A reframe or new interpretation thus becomes possible, and with it, different feelings and different action alternatives.

Chapter 5

FAMILY DEVELOPMENT THROUGH THE LIFE CYCLE

> ...the developmental conceptual frame-
> work... brings together from rural socio-
> logists the idea of stages of the life cycle,
> from child psychologists and human devel-
> opment researchers concepts of develop-
> mental needs and tasks, from the sociolo-
> gy of the professions the idea of a family
> as a set of mutually contingent careers,
> and from the structure function and inter-
> action theorists such concepts as age and
> sex roles, plurality patterns, functional
> prerequisites, and other concepts which
> view the family as a system of interacting
> actors.
>
> Rueben Hill and Roy H. Rodgers

Viewing the family as a system requires that we look at the whole and at the dynamic interaction of individual members. We understand that relationships are characterized by rules or redundant patterns of interaction. We find that because of such redundant patterns families may arrive at identical situations even though they have started out in many different ways. We recognize that the redundant patterns form boundaries which separate systems from one another. And we realize that a balance between stability and change is preferable for the attainment of a well functioning family.

We might say that the family maintains stability through change appropriate to the developmental stages of individual members and of the system as a whole. Thus we juxtapose the orderly direction of change in a framework that enables predictability within the concept of system.

Indeed, knowledge of developmental stages is useful for families in order that they may take appropriate action when necessary and may avoid overreacting when little or no action is required (Watzlawick, Weakland & Fisch, 1974). A functional family evolves relative to both external and internal pressures. It also has an interpretive system which is sufficiently informed so that change at the appropriate time in appropriate amounts is anticipated and accommodated. In other words, there are rules for changing the rules.

For example, a family may come into therapy for help with a child who is having problems in school. The therapist would do well to consider the ages of the parents and the child as well as the position of the child in the family. For therapy is likely to be more productive if attention is paid to the developmental issues of both individual members and of the family as a whole.

Indeed, both individuals and families may be conceptualized as proceeding through developmental cycles in which different stages are characterized by different sources of conflict and solidarity. And although there are a variety of theoretical frameworks dealing with the patterns of growth and development, we would like to discuss two which we have found to be particularly useful.

The key to Erikson's (1963) eight stage theory of individual development and the life cycle lies in the concept of the attainment of "inner sameness and continuity" by a progression through developmental stages, each of which has specific tasks with which the individual must deal, with each stage building upon the one that preceded it. According to Erikson, "psychosocial development proceeds by critical stages - 'critical' being a characteristic of turning points, of moments of decision between progress and regression, integration and retardation" (1963, pp. 270-271). The individual is thus seen as a creative being who is faced with particular challenges at particular points in life, and society is viewed as responding to maintain the proper progression for this "succession of potentialities." The following chart presents Erikson's eight stages and the developmental tasks appropriate to each according to his framework:

ERIK ERIKSON'S "EIGHT AGES OF MAN"

	Stage	Developmental Task
I.	Oral-Sensory	Basic Trust vs. Mistrust
II.	Muscular-Anal	Autonomy vs. Shame and Doubt
III.	Locomotor-Genital	Initiative vs. Guilt
IV.	Latency	Industry vs. Inferiority
V.	Puberty and Adolescence	Identity vs. Role Confusion
VI.	Young Adulthood	Intimacy vs. Isolation
VII.	Adulthood	Generativity vs. Stagnation
VIII.	Maturity	Ego Integrity vs. Despair

This framework describes stages of individual development. Viewed systemically, the family is the context in which these developmental tasks are or are not mastered. A functional family provides a context in which each family member masters appropriate developmental tasks and is thus prepared to interface successfully with other systems.

Similarly, we can also describe a stage critical family life cycle schema which broadens our understanding of the family system at any given point in time. A summary of this model is presented by means of the following chart:

STAGES OF THE FAMILY LIFE CYCLE*

Stage	Emotion Issues	Stage Critical Tasks
1. The Unattached Adult	Accepting parent-offspring separation.	a. Differentiation from family of origin. b. Development of peer relations. c. Initiation of career.
2. Newly Married Couple	Commitment to the marriage.	a. Formation of marital system. b. Taking on parenting roles. c. Making room for spouse with family and friends.
3. Childbearing	Accepting new members into the system.	a. Adjusting marriage to make room. b. taking on parenting roles. c. Making room for grandparents.
4. Preschool-Age Child	Accepting the new personality.	a. Adjusting family systems to needs of a specific child. b. Coping with energy drain and lack of privacy.

(*From Barnhill & Longo, 1978; Carter & McGoldrick, 1980; Duvall, 1977.)

Stage	Emotion Issues	Stage Critical Tasks
5. School-Age Child	Allowing child to establish relationships outside the family.	a. Extending family system to interact with society. b. Encouraging child's educational achievement.
6. Teenage Child	Increasing flexibility of family boundaries to allow child's independence.	a. Shifting parent-child relationship to balance freedom/limits. b. Refocusing on mid-life career and marital issues. c. Beginning concerns for older generation.
7. Launching Center	Accepting exits from and entries into the family.	a. Releasing young adult children into work, college, marriage. b. Maintaining a supportive home base.
8. Middle-Age Parents	Letting go and facing each other again.	a. Rebuilding the marriage. b. Realigning family to include spouses of children and grandchildren. c. Dealing with aging of one's own parents.
9. Retirement	Accepting retirement and old age.	a. Adjusting to retirement. b. Coping with death of parents, spouse. c. Closing or adapting family house. d. Maintaining individual and couple functioning. e. Supporting middle generation.

By using the two conceptualizations just outlined in combination, we are able to understand the individual in terms of the process of growth and development, to see him or her in the context of his or her family at any given point in its developmental process, and to anticipate the normal issues with which families in general must contend as they grow and evolve.

Therefore, let us take a brief look at the life cycle of a hypothetical family, considering the processes of system formation and evolution over time. Although we will not dwell on problem formation or resolution, we will attempt to describe the kinds of intertwining issues and troublesome transition points at which families may easily get stuck. Although not the case with this family, it is at such points that we often see families in therapy. Hence the necessity for understanding the complexity of family growth and development.

As you will recall from our chart, Stage 1 in the family life cycle is that of the unattached adult. The emotion issues center around the acceptance of parent-offspring separation. The stage critical tasks include differentiation from family of origin, the development of peer relations and the initiation of a career. From Erikson's framework we also have the issue of intimacy vs. isolation. Thus we first encounter the relationship system of Ted and Carol, aged 27 and 25 respectively.

Having taken the first steps in the process of separating from their families of origin, both are involved with beginning careers and with the formation of a stable and meaningful relationship with one another. Ted is in graduate school, completing his M. B. A., and he works part time as a check-out clerk at a nearby grocery store. Carol has a degree in elementary education and teaches third grade in a neighboring district.

After college Carol had shared an apartment with two other girls. Ted lived at home during his undergraduate years but took an apartment nearer the campus when he began graduate school. During his final year of study, the couple decided to live together. This was a time of adjustment as Ted and Carol were now interacting on a daily basis and were struggling to harmonize the relationship rules which each had brought from his or her family of origin. And although they lived in an environment that was accepting of their life style, the messages received and processed from their respective families were not as favorable.

Carol's parents had a particularly difficult time accepting and understanding how to relate to Ted and their daughter in the context of this living arrangement. They saw a deviation from the family rules and gave feedback aimed at returning the system to its previous state. Thus the families of origin were a part of the relationship system of Ted and Carol.

The couple is now in the process of evolving a comfortable and acceptable pattern of interaction for their relationship within the context of their environment. And deciding that they wish to make a permanent commitment to one another, they plan to marry as soon as Ted is graduated and finds a job.

When next we encounter Ted and Carol it is as a newly married couple who are dealing with the Stage 2 emotion issue of commitment to the marriage. Their critical tasks for this phase of the family life cycle include formation of the marital system and making room for the spouse with family and friends. They have resolved the developmental task of young adulthood to some extent by making the choice of marriage. The degree to which they successfully complete this task will be reflected in the degree of intimacy they are able to achieve in their marital relationship.

Although the couple had expected little or no difference in their relationship, they soon find that marriage is a very different context and the transition proves to be somewhat difficult. Each has new expectations of the other brought from their families of origin. As a married couple they experience and are experienced differently in their social environment, which gradually expands and becomes a context for new pressures as there are greater inputs of information into the system. And with the legalization of their relationship they find themselves more involved with their inlaws as each maintains a role within his or her respective family of origin.

Ted and Carol have agreed that both will work for at least three more years before starting a family. They continue to be involved in establishing their careers. They are able to put away some money for the future and still have sufficient income to live comfortably. The rules of their relationship provide time to be both together and apart, either with friends or alone. In time they work out a relationship of mutual support so that they can complete routine tasks and still have time to play together.

The couple enjoy going camping and hiking, and summer vacations are sometimes spent backpacking or mountain climbing. During the week both are busy with their jobs but each finds the other interesting to talk to and be with during their times alone. They evolve a circle of friends that they are comfortable visiting with from time to time and they keep in touch with their families at least once a week. All in all, a fairly stable pattern.

As they near the end of the second year of marriage, Carol and Ted begin to receive increased numbers of messages from both sets of parents about the importance of grandchildren and about how they shouldn't wait too long before becoming parents. Although they consider the possibility of changing their plans, they ultimately agree to wait and it isn't until about a year and a half later that they decide to have their first child.

However, Carol does not become pregnant immediately and decides to continue working. Ted, meanwhile begins to rise in the business world, and with increases in both their salaries they decide to buy a home of their own. They find it difficult to reconcile their different tastes in picking and furnishing a house, but eventually are able to reach acceptable compromises. All of these events represent developmental crises, or challenges, and as such are potential sources of problems. But Ted and Carol have sufficient flexibility to evolve new rules for their relationship as needed and we soon find them moving into the next stage of the family life cycle.

Stage 3 is the childbearing stage and the emotion issue is that of accepting new members into the system. Adjusting the marriage to make room for children, taking on parenting roles, and making room for grandparents comprise the stage critical tasks. The individual development stage is that of adulthood and the task that of generativity vs. stagnation both in terms of procreation, and creativity in one's chosen field of endeavor.

Ted and Carol had not been in their new home a year before their first child was born. Although each is very excited about their baby daughter, Ann, they have some misgivings about their ability to be good parents and are daily becoming more aware of the increased complexity of their little family. Carol is concerned about whether or not to become a full time mother and therefore decides to take a maternity leave rather than quitting her job entirely. Ted is not happy with this decision and it is the subject of many heated discussions.

Ted is also resentful of the amount of time which Carol must devote to the baby and he begins to stay out late a couple of nights a week. Carol is tired from all her new activities and becomes upset by what she feels is Ted's lack of interest in the baby. And both must figure out how to handle diplomatically the well-meaning but often intrusive behaviors of the new grandparents.

Eventually Carol and Ted are able to work out a new relationship which gives them time to be a couple as well as parents. Carol decides to resign her teaching position and two years later they have a second child, another daughter, whom they name Ellen. Having successfully weathered the crises of parenthood which accompanied the birth of Ann, they are better able to handle the increasing complexity of their four member family system.

As the children grow into toddlers we now encounter the family in Stage 4 of the family life cycle. With preschool-age children they must accept the new personality of each of their offspring. The family's tasks include adjusting the system to the needs of the children and coping with the energy drain and lack of privacy as a married couple. Individually, the children must deal first with the developmental tasks of basic trust vs. mistrust followed by autonomy vs. shame and doubt and the family must provide a context for the successful resolution of these tasks. As adults Ted and Carol continue to be concerned with the issue of generativity vs. stagnation.

Carol now begins to evolve a new network of relationships as she becomes better acquainted with the other parents of young children living in their neighborhood. And as she learns to structure and schedule daily routines for herself and the children, she finds time to become involved in local politics and begins taking piano lessons, the fulfillment of some long time dreams. Ted continues to be very occupied with his job, which he finds stimulating and challenging. And he spends time with his wife and daughters as he is able.

Although their worlds are very different now, Ted and Carol feel that their relationship is quite satisfactory. They are proud of their little family despite some ups and downs which they consider to be fairly normal.

The family moves to Stage 5 as first Ann and then Ellen goes off to school. With school-age children, the emotion issue involves allowing each child to establish relationships outside the family. The stage critical tasks involve extending the family system to interact with society and encouraging each child's educational achievement. Generativity vs. stagnation continue to be developmental concerns of our adult parents, while for the children, industry vs. inferiority is the task at hand.

The children move into school with little difficulty and Carol, who is at first saddened by Ellen's eagerness to go off with her sister each morning, begins to enjoy the extra time for herself. Afternoons after school become exciting times as the girls describe their day's activity for their mother. It is then homework time and Ann and Ellen work at the kitchen table. Carol usually sits with them, reading a book or giving some assistance when it is needed.

Both Ted and Carol are interested in their children's educational activity. They join the parent-teachers association and go together to parent conferences whenever possible. When difficulties arise in school they feel fortunate that they are familiar with the various teachers and school routines.

As the children make new friends and become more involved in outside activities, Carol faces a crisis in terms of role adjustment. She no longer feels totally satisfied staying at home all day. She therefore begins to think about returning to work, believing that the family could probably manage if household activities were well planned.

Thus when Ann and Ellen enter the sixth and fourth grades respectively, Carol returns to teaching third grade, this time in the same school that her children attend. The three of them go back and forth to school together, so babysitting is not a problem. However, Carol now has much less time at home and it becomes necessary to make some adjustments in job assignments.

Ted and Carol take turns preparing dinner and doing other major household chores such as laundry, cleaning and gardening. The girls are given jobs appropriate to their ages and everyone is expected to pitch in as needed. Needless to say, this reorganization does not occur without a certain amount of interpersonal tension and upset. Gradually, however, the family is able to establish a routine which includes not only work but also time for play both together and separately. And Ted and Carol take time to enjoy each other without the children.

We next find the family in Stage 6 as Ann and Ellen reach adolescence. With teenage children, the family emotion issue is that of increasing the flexibility of the family boundaries in order to provide a context in which Ann and Ellen can make more decisions for themselves. The stage critical tasks include shifting the parent-child relationship to balance freedom and limits, refocusing on midlife career and marital issues and beginning concerns for the older generation. For the adolescent, identity vs. role confusion is a major issue, and for the parents of adolescents it is a time of assessment in terms of how far one has come and how far it is still possible to go in one's life and career.

Ann and Ellen are on their own now as each attends different schools. With Ann in high school, Ellen in junior high school and Carol teaching at the elementary school, everyone is on a different schedule. Ted and Carol find themselves having to change the rules for the girls in response to normal developmental pressures. At the same time, Ann and Ellen are recognizing their limits as well as the increase in responsibility that comes with an increase in "freedom."

Meanwhile, Ted has begun to question his job and to struggle with doubts about the kind of success he can reasonably expect in his chosen career. He considers the possibility of taking several different positions, occasionally going out on job interviews. He spends a great deal of time alone and begins to feel as though he is losing contact with his family. Although they try to be understanding of his struggle, each is also involved with her own issues.

Another crisis occurs around Carol's parents. Although Ted's parents are handling retirement well, Carol's mother and father are both in ill health and Carol is attempting to help care for them as well as work and be available for her husband and children. Although she tries to be supportive of Ted, she realizes that she is not as effective as she would like to be and in turn longs for more support from Ted with her own burdens.

We will leave the family at this point, returning somewhat later to find them in Stage 7. This stage is termed the launching center and the emotion issue is that of accepting exists from and entries into the family. The tasks involve releasing young adult children into work, college, marriage, etc., and maintaining a supportive home base. Individually, each family member is in the later phases of the developmental tasks encountered in Stage 6 of the family life cycle.

Carol and Ted find it hard to believe that so many years have passed as they take Ann to college for the first time. It is a happy-sad time, for they are aware that their older daughter is essentially leaving home for good and will no longer be their little girl. Ellen also finds it fun to be an "only child," but often rebels at having to take over some of Ann's jobs around the house. Once again, routines have to be adjusted, but eventually life becomes a little less hectic with only three different schedules to coordinate.

Ted and Carol begin to spend more time together and are able to support one another when Carol's parents die and Ted's parents move to a retirement community and they have to close up the family homes. Ted has decided to make a lateral move within his company to a more interesting position, and tries to go fishing on the weekend whenever he can.

Occasionally the couple go camping as they had when they were younger and they use the time to talk, sometimes about the possibility of Carol's going to graduate school. Carol has decided that she would like to become a school counselor and plans to begin work on a master's degree sometime in the future. She decides to wait until both girls are well into college and the family can more easily afford the cost of another tuition.

Once both girls are in college, Carol and Ted find they enjoy both their increased solitude as well as the occasional noise and confusion which reign when Ann and Ellen come home for vacations, often bringing friends with them. The family also has some difficulties in blending life styles inasmuch as Ann and Ellen have become accustomed to living according to different sets of rules.

When Ann graduates from college, she moves to another city where she has found a job working on a newspaper. She visits her parents occasionally and is often in touch by phone. She is happy with her new life and quickly develops a new circle of friends.

Carol now begins graduate school on a part-time basis while continuing to work. She and Ellen, a junior in college, often compare notes on student life. Ted is pleased with Carol's choice but misses the time they had had to do things together. Carol has to spend many hours attending class and studying. Ted tries to pitch in with more of the housework, but he looks forward to the day when Carol will return to a more predictable routine.

Ted has recently received a promotion which brought with it both a higher salary and the necessity to do some traveling. He would like Carol to be able to go with him on some of these trips. Carol, however, is very involved in her graduate work as well as the demands of her job and doesn't feel free to go with Ted.

When Ellen graduates from college and moves into town, Carol quits her teaching job and goes to school on a full-time basis. Within a year she is able to complete her master's degree in counseling. At the same time, Ann has decided to marry and the family finds itself in the middle of marriage preparations as well as in the process of moving into the next stage of their family life cycle.

Stage 8 is the stage of middle-age parents who must let go of their children and face each other again. Their tasks are to rebuild their marriage as a two person system, to realign their family to include spouses of children and grandchildren and to deal with their own aging parents. Their children are now young adults making choices around intimacy vs. isolation, and as they enter the individual stage of maturity, Ted and Carol will need to deal with the task of ego integrity vs. despair.

Carol and Ted are fond of their new son-in-law and they look forward to the day when they will become grandparents. However, remembering their own experience, they do not talk to Ann and her new husband about this subject. They find it an interesting challenge to readjust their thinking about their children now that they are adults. Ellen is enjoying success as a public relations consultant and is intent on pursuing a career, a decision about which her parents have some mixed emotions.

Having returned to the status of married couple without dependent children, Ted and Carol are in the process of renewing their relationship. Carol has taken a part-time job which gives her some flexibility to travel with Ted. They enjoy having Ann and her husband for dinner once in a while and most of their contact with Ellen is by phone.

During this period, Ted's father dies and the family decides that Ted's mother will come and live with them. Although everyone is in favor of this choice, it requires some adjustment to have another person living in the house. However, Ted's mother is able to help out around the house, which enhances her sense of usefulness, and Carol appreciates the assistance. They all manage to give each other enough space so that their interactions generally tend to be harmonious.

We come now to the final stage in the family life cycle. Retirement characterizes Stage 9, and accepting retirement and old age is its emotion issue. Adjusting to retirement, coping with the death of parents and/or spouse, closing or adapting the family house, providing support for a more central role of the middle generation, and maintaining their functioning as individuals and as a couple comprise the stage critical tasks for Ted and Carol. This latter task relates to the final resolution of the issue of ego integrity vs. despair with which each began to deal in the previous stage. For their children, the developmental tasks revolve around intimacy vs. isolation and generativity vs. stagnation. And Ann and Ellen are both also interacting in terms of the appropriate stage of their own family life cycles.

Ted decides to retire early, and not long afterward his mother dies. He and Carol now are concerned with the question of how they will spend their remaining years together. Ted would like to sell their house and move to a warmer climate, but Carol prefers to continue working for a few more years and is not anxious to move away from her children.

Ted and Carol agree that they will remain where they are for the time being and Ted finds part-time work as a consultant. He is soon busy again meeting a new series of challenges and finds the people with whom he is working interesting and enjoyable. He and Carol also begin to take weekend trips to the mountains they used to enjoy climbing. And they continue the process of evolving family rules in response to information from within and without their relationship system as they complete their journey through the family life cycle.

As we have attempted to illustrate with the foregoing, each of the events within the life cycle, both individual and family, requires a modification of roles and of the rules of the relationships among family members. As mentioned previously, it is at the points of transition that problems are most likely to arise. Thus, if an event occurs without the appropriate modification in response to that event, a crisis may result. In systems terms, we would say that the negative feedback will escalate in ever more dysfunctional patterns. The system would therefore be moving toward greater chaos, or entropy, as it failed to incorporate new information in a manner consistent with movement toward greater complexity and flexibility, or negative entropy.

Similarly, inappropriate action taken to modify the structure which is otherwise evolving normally may precipitate a crisis within the family. For example, the adolescent needs of Ann and Ellen for greater freedom were normal and to be expected. However, if Ted and Carol had looked upon the expression of these needs as "teenage rebellion" and responded accordingly, the family would in all likelihood have found itself locked in conflict. On the other hand, since the family anticipated such needs by offering opportunities for the exercise of greater freedom on the part of their adolescents, many problems were avoided and the system provided a context which fostered both individual and family development.

Indeed, another way of considering the impact of developmental stages within and upon families is to view them from the perspective of the way in which freedom is managed in a family. According to Bender (1976), stringent restrictions of the very young child gradually give way to almost complete freedom at the time when the young adult is ready to leave home. A rather authoritarian mode of behavior on the part of the parent may therefore be functional when children are quite small. However, this mode needs to be revised with the increase in intellectual and moral development of the child. Thus, "Sit down!" to a four year old may become, "You seem quite restless and impatient," to a fifteen year old. Ideally commands are replaced by reason and persuasion, or meta-communication, as the individual matures.

As the family moves through its life cycle, it must be able to anticipate an increase in individuation and variation as members interface with more and more diverse systems. A family needs continually to reorganize in the process of maintaining itself, and must increase in complexity to allow for change without self-destruction. Ever increasing amounts of information must be processed by the system. The boundaries must be open to inputs from a variety of new and different systems and yet must be sufficiently defined so that family identity is preserved. Paradoxically, family cohesion is probably best achieved by allowing individuality and variation commensurate to the developmental stages of individual members and thus of the family as a whole.

In addition to normal developmental patterns, unexpected events may also challenge the family and necessitate appropriate action either to modify the structure or maintain the status quo. For example, the death of a family member must be considered in terms of its effect on the relationships and the role structure in the family. As pointed out by Bossard (1945), an arithmetic increase or decrease in the number of members in a primary group is accompanied by a corresponding geometric increase or decrease in the number of relationships in that group. The death or loss of one member in a family of five would therefore mean a reduction in the number of relationships from ten to six.

Similarly, adaptation of family structure is also appropriate when a gradually deteriorating marriage ends in divorce. The family must regroup itself by assuming roles and rules for relationships which are consistent with the change in the system. When the children are living with one parent, they and the other parent will need to relate to each other in a manner different from when the family was living together. The parent with custody will need to institute new rules in order to achieve and maintain stability in the newly constituted family. And the divorced parents will need to evolve a set of rules appropriate for their new relationship.

Likewise, sickness of a family member, unemployment of a significant breadwinner, sudden acquisition of wealth, an encounter with the courts, etc., all require responses to either modify or maintain the structure according to the new demands upon the system. Further, since it is at the points of transition that families are most susceptible to problem formation, one needs to be aware of the number of stress-producing events impinging upon the system at any given time and recognize that the capacity of the family to cope adaptively will be affected accordingly.

Finally, we must briefly consider the family in the context of society. Certainly the family has received much abuse and has been much discussed, often in despairing terms, in recent years. However, we believe that the fact that the family has been able to adapt and persist, both in more traditional forms and in the so-called variant forms, and thus has succeeded in responding to a variety of changes within its suprasystem while still remaining a highly viable entity is a measure of its great strength.

Far from being "broken down," the family has become a complex system of systems with many different forms. Boundaries have been expanded, new rules for family life have been tested and in some cases have been tentatively accepted. Indeed, the family has become much more highly evolved as it interacts with other systems in an increasingly more complex society.

We therefore also believe that the most threatening posture to assume is one that defines the family as being in trouble or as having a problem. For just as is the case in any system that it is often the behavior around a so-called problem which is the problem, so it may be our attitude and behavior toward the family that is problematic.

There has indeed been a great increase in the rate of divorce in our society of late, and the last several decades have been a period of enormous change for both individuals and families. Many have turned elsewhere, possibly in an attempt to find something that was missing in their families. But while divorce, separation, and the loss of a parent are most commonly negative experiences, in reality the consequences of such events usually result in reorganization rather than breakdown. The family still remains a family, albeit one without a father or a mother, or one with a different form. And if one looks at the experimentation, rebellion and challenges to traditional norms and values as being part of a normal developmental process of family systems, the existence of these behaviors may be seen in a new, less threatening light.

The family is uniquely suited for providing a legitimate context for intimacy and for passing on society's values to succeeding generations. And rather than assuming that the family is in a process of entropy, perhaps it would be more useful for us to recognize its strengths as well as its weaknesses as it struggles for a new identity in a time of great transitions.

We might do well to consider the increasingly complex set of values which characterize our society and thus recognize the increase in new information which the family must process in its daily interactions. We might benefit by understanding the evolution of this system as it moves toward greater complexity consistent with its environment. And we might also conceptualize the family as being in an adolescent stage of development, not unlike the society of which it is a part (Bender, 1976). Such an approach might then lead not only to an awareness of the family's limitations but also to respect for its vigor and potential. One might then also argue that in time this "rebellious youth" will in all likelihood mature into an even more responsible "adult," capable of making ever greater contributions to the societal system of which it is a part. One way of interacting effectively with this formidable adolescent might be to give the family greater attention from a developmental rather than from a therapeutic perspective. Thus might we as family therapists be a part of the solution rather than of the problem.

Chapter 6

THE FAMILY AS SYSTEM

> Systems theory has evolved in response to
> plural and often mutually exclusive inter-
> pretations of the world, and has spent
> most of its energies on making an impor-
> tant point, namely that there is another,
> perhaps more integrated way of looking
> at things.
>
> Michael Seidler

The family is a human system consisting of the interactions among father,
mother (whether both is physically present or not) and children. One hypothesis is that members of the marital dyad are attracted to each other on the
basis of the perceived compatibility of the rule system each brings from his
or her family of origin. Portions of these rule systems are combined according to the need for maintaining the new system in a balance between stability and change. Rules within a family may be thought of as being on a continuum from explicit, or closer to the awareness of family members, to implicit, or outside the awareness of family members but able to be inferred from
its redundant patterns.

Observations of a family in action reveal repetitive interaction patterns
among family members. These patterns can be construed as unspoken agree-
ments which define various relationships in the family. They circumscribe
the manner in which family members communicate with each other, the nature of the relationships between family members, and how decisions are
made in the family. These rules create a stable, predictable system which
is resistant to change. Rule systems tend to be passed on from one generation
to the next with only slight modifications.

The boundary of the family system is the discrimination which family
members make between "ours" and events out there-- other families, other

people, other things. The boundary of the family is less distinct in its formation stages and becomes progressively clearer as the family matures. Even in maturity, however, a family's boundary may be modified to include more or less of the family's surroundings, although the rules for inclusion or exclusion remain relatively stable.

The components of the family system are its members and the relationships which exist between and among family members. Family members have perceptions, cognitions, affections, and acts of which each is aware as belonging to "family." The family system refers to interpersonal processes, and these processes are assumed to be somewhat predictable, and as such fall within the domain of scientific inquiry.

The family is a separate system which accepts inputs from without (exteroceptive) and from within (interoceptive). These inputs are processed and the system emits acts or behaviors as outputs. The inputs within the family are the communication patterns which define each relationship within the family as distinct from every other relationship, and each individual as distinct from every other individual. The particular assemblage of individuals who relate to each other in fairly predictable ways, which are distinct from any other system outside the family, define the family as different from all other families. The family is also a subsystem of a larger suprasystem.

The family is characterized by a degree of stability and integration. This does not mean the family is rigid over time, but that one of its proper - ties is a tendency toward equilibrium within a framework of growth, or morphostasis. Because the ongoing activities of the family system are organized and integrated in relation to the system itself, each family system tends to establish a relatively consistent life style. Families have characteristic ways of doing, thinking, reacting and growing which tend to distinguish them from every other family. Thus, the family puts its personal stamp on each role it plays and each situation it encounters. The family is fairly consistent in regarding others as either honest or untrustworthy, in perceiving life as either exciting or threatening, or perhaps as a constant struggle, in seeking certain experiences and avoiding others.

A family's typical patterns of behavior are consistent with that family's interpretive system, values and self-definition. A family defines itself and its members according to the metaphors it employs to describe itself in the context of various situations and experiences.

When confronted with situations or experiences that are not in accord with the family's value system, feedback processes which seek to temper, adapt, minimize or preclude this information come into play. The net outcome of these feedback processes is the assurance of the continuation of the family's value system as it is manifested in its interaction patterns and in its life style.

If the family system is markedly out of accord with its environment and rejects all inputs, the behavior of the family or its members may conflict with other systems in that environment. Similarly, if the behavior of an individual within the family is markedly out of accord with the family's values and interaction style, the individual may conflict with others within the family.

Family systems operate to produce useful and useless outputs, the criterion of usefulness being established by systems outside the family or by the suprasystem. Problem families, i.e., families poorly adapted to their milieu or whose activities produce individuals who are poorly adapted to their milieu in one respect or another, become dysfunctional through the operation of the same basic family development principles that apply to non-problem families. No family attains a perfectly satisfactory or optimal adaptation; all families produce some "error."

Families are neither "good" nor "bad." They are so labeled by some other system. When the interface of a family with its suprasystem occurs with only tolerable error, the family is said to be reasonably well adjusted. Within the family, when the interface of family members with each other occurs with only tolerable error, the family may view itself and its members as reasonably well adapted.

Chapter 7

A CRITIQUE AND DEFENSE OF THE SYSTEMS PERSPECTIVE

> We may never know whether the 'real'
> world, the ultimate reality which surely
> underlies all our observations and cons-
> titutes our very existence is truly ordered,
> and if so, whether it is divided into dis-
> tinct types of special order or manifests
> one overarching systematic order. What
> we do know is that the human mind seeks
> order and that the more general and sim-
> ple the order it discriminates the more
> meaning it confers on experience. As
> long as no direct metaphysical insights
> into the nature of reality are available,
> we must reconstruct reality through ra-
> tional theories with empirical applica-
> tions.
>
> Ervin Laszlo

The systems perspective would have us see individuals <u>relatively</u>, or relative to context, rather than substantively, or as particular types of individuals having particular psychological traits, or being a certain way. Thus
Steve is not a specific sort of fellow; rather, he is a certain kind of person
with me the way I am with him, or in this context.

Relativism requires that we see reciprocity or circularity in relationships
rather than linear cause and effect. The most powerful interpersonal language directs our attention to interfacing rather than to intentionality in one
another. That is, "We really get on each other's nerves," rather than, "you
always make me angry," or, "you are a rotten person."

System, or relativistic diagnosis assumes that the behavior of each defines both the self and the other in a relationship in terms of a given context.
When I teach and you attend my lecture we are defined in the context of the
classroom as professor and students. We assume reciprocal roles to one another and interact accordingly:

53

None of us could maintain these behaviors for very long in the absence of their logical complement.

I cannot continue to behave, feel and think in a manner appropriate to the role of teacher unless someone takes a reciprocal or complementary role, i.e., feeds back to me through his or her behavior that he/she takes the command implicit in my teaching behavior and is a student. The systems model would have us see this reciprocal influence in all social systems, and it suggests that a given role cannot maintain itself of its own energy. Rather, its maintenance requires another role which is logically complementary to it.

The influence of two persons in a relationship is mutual. Therefore, both are responsible and yet neither is responsible. Each may seek to establish unilateral control of a relationship, but each is doomed to fail in such an effort, for a relationship is bilateral by definition. As we cannot not communicate, we cannot not influence the relationships of which we are a part. Interdependence is the rule within a systems framework and independence and dependence have meaning only as we redefine them with reference to a given context.

The persons in a relationship are both free and controlled; that is, free to the extent that they recognize the limits of the contract that they have evolved. Because of the bilateral nature of the interaction in a relationship, attempts to change the relationship contract are best done by bilateral agreement. While attempts at one-upsmanship are not precluded, they may lead to dissolution of the relationship unless such attempts are transformed into a bilateral effort. When dissolution of a relationship is precluded, as in a parent-child dyad, failure to adjust the context in response to feedback which indicates a problem may lead to a continually deteriorating relationship. This is reflected in an increasing frequency and amplification of the behavior that was originally deemed undesirable and was the target for change.

The concepts presented as basic to a systems perspective lay the groundwork for an ecological epistemology. Such a perspective is quite different from the individual vs. environment viewpoint. The systems model does not view the individual vs. environment issue as a useful question. It accepts both as important elements and acknowledges the reciprocal relationship between the two. Further, in the systems model neither can be meaningfully understood without the other, for the environment is not viewed as something in opposition to the individual but rather is inclusive of him or her. The individual is neither the all-powerful self-determining person nor the pawn. The question of whether the individual or the environment is more powerful is not meaningful in a systems framework. Mutual influence is the rule, and the interface between individuals and systems provides the key to understanding their relationship.

We believe that the fact that human beings create theories testifies to their genius and uniqueness as the only known organisms who are able to conceptualize their own experience. A systems theory is but one example of this genius. It presents a view of the world in which individuals are seen in a collaborative and cooperative relationship with all other members and aspects of their environment rather than envisioning a world of protagonistic-antagonistic forces.

The systems perspective is, we believe a useful explanation of reality. Its generality and applicability to a wide variety of phenomena, however, can be seen as having both assets and liabilities. On the one hand, explanations from this perspective can be so all-encompassing and concepts so broad that we are precluded from action. For example, carried to the extreme, a systems perspective would have us see Steve in relation to other persons and systems such as family, peers, work group, church members, etc.,
> who are part of a community system;
> which is part of a societal system;
> which is part of a cultural system;
> which is part of a national system;
> which is part of a world system;
> which is part of the cosmic system;
>> of which the viewer is also a part.

When we see the interrelatedness of these several systems, each of which is a part of, and to some extent influences the other, we might be led to believe that in order to effectively help Steve we would have to involve ourselves with each of the other systems impinging upon him. Thus, if we take the model to its limits, we may be moved to inaction, and possibly to despair. For, carried to the extreme, a systems perspective is indeed too general to be useful. However, this generality does not necessarily prevent our taking action. If we are able to focus on those systems which contribute most heavily to the maintenance of Steve's dysfunctional state, then the problem assumes more manageable proportions.

There seems to be abundant empirical evidence to suggest that the family system exerts the greatest influence on an individual, followed by other systems such as school, church, and work, which impact upon the family. These, we maintain, are within the range of our ability to influence as we attempt to help Steve. Further, this does not mean that Steve cannot be helped apart from these systems.

A fundamental premise of the helping professions is that an individual can be helped in a relationship or system with a counselor, and the subsequent change will affect other systems of which that individual is also a member. For example, a change in Steve, if maintained, will have ramifications for his family, work, church,and peer relationships. Because of his new ways of interacting within these systems, Steve, once changed, will set off a ripple of change in a manner not unlike a pebble tossed into a pond. That this can happen is well documented and is in no way inconsistent with the systems model; in fact, it validates this perspective.

From a systems perspective, "mental health" can be seen as relationship health. According to this viewpoint, the counselor's goals include primary prevention activities, or relationship development, in the form of marriage and family development and enrichment, as well as relationship remediation and rehabilitation, or marriage and family therapy. This model also suggests that when viewed in the context of a particular relationship, behavior labeled as "mental illness" may make sense, or may logically fit the context.

As we draw on the more general systems perspective, we can create a model for a functional system. As is so often the case, the issue seems to be that of achieving a balance between extremes:

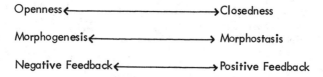

The desired balance between two extremes does not necessarily depreciate the value of either extreme as a functional pattern to fit a particular situation. Indeed, a functional set of relationships within a family will contain behaviors that exemplify both extremes. However, over time, the family will tend to blend the two extremes into a balance. Yet a limited balance is probably not sufficient. What probably is essential is the capacity of a family to make decisions to shift or strike a balance at the appropriate time in the appropriate context.

It is our hypothesis that no functional relationship system can remain effective if it exists for extended periods of time at either end of the continuum. The desired balance was described well in The Prophet by Kahlil Gibran (1923):

> Sing and dance together and be joyous,
>   but let each one of you be alone

Even as the strings of a lute are alone
   though they quiver with the same music
And stand together yet not too near together;
For the pillars of the temple stand apart,
And the oak tree and the cypress grow
   not in each other's shadow
But let there be spaces in your togetherness
And let the winds of the heavens dance between you.

Thus, we see our task as marriage and family therapists and as family development consultants and parent educators as that of helping families attain the balance: to be stable and yet be able to change; to be open selectively; to allow for individuation and inclusion; to understand relatedness and interdependence. To know how to decide what to do, when, is the key. A part of this challenge is to teach people to think of their relationships relatively rather than substantively so that they can recognize a basic premise of systems theory, i.e., that one influences while being influenced, that Sue is not a person who "is upset," but that she, "is upset with me the way I am with her."

On the other hand, while we accept systems theory as a very useful model and as an applied framework in the field of therapy, we would feel remiss if we did not recognize that like most theories, it is not without its episte - mological problems or paradoxes. Three paradoxes in general systems theory have been described (Sadovsky, 1974). These concern hierarchicality, wholeness, and methodology.

The problem of hierarchicality involves the paradox of being able to define system "a" as being a component of a larger system "A". This we cannot do unless system "a" can first be defined as a system. As Seidler (1979) noted, there is a mutual interdependence of the two problems, each of which must be solved first in order to solve the other, hence the paradox.

A second paradox rests with the concept of wholeness. In order to be able to describe a system as a whole, we must be able to break it down into parts. Breaking the system down into parts requires first that we be able to describe it as a whole. As with hierarchicality, "... the interdependence of two problems precludes the solution of either, and so of both." (Seidler, 1979, p. 48).

Systems methodology is the subject of the third paradox. As with any discipline, the problem concerns the answer to a chicken and egg question. Did we first have the methodology which enabled us to attain a degree of knowledge based upon which we made certain assumptions; or based upon our knowledge of systems did we formulate a methodology which in turn is essential to our having that knowledge?

Epistemological problems like the paradoxes just described are not unique to the systems model by any means. Paradoxes generated by knowledge claims occur in all theories in all disciplines. For example, the concept of the unconscious is by definition unknowable within the theory that invents it. Similarly, the empiricist tradition asserts that a knowledge claim is acceptable only through data accessible to our senses. One might ask of this assertion, where is the sensory data that allows this statement as a valid knowledge claim?

We recognize that there are no solutions possible for such epistemological problems given man's inability to transcend himself. And while such problems may render a model no less useful in reality, we feel it is important to point out their existence. Further, while our task as theory-builders is to create a theory that is self-referentially consistent, i.e., does not contain knowledge claims that are contradicted from within by its own constructs, we must not fall into the trap of believing that our theories are greater than they are. We believe it is to the credit of systems theorists that they have recognized the epistemological problems in their model. As Bertalanffy noted:

> The various systems sciences have shown that there
> are concepts, models and invariants revealing a
> general order that transcends the more or less special
> ones in the conventional sciences. Let us be aware
> that this too is a 'perspective of reality', determined
> and limited by our human bondage. But so after all,
> are also conventional and orthodox disciplines.
> (Bertalanffy, 1972, p. 145)

Chapter 8

IMPLICATIONS FOR FAMILY THERAPY

> Shifting one's thinking from the individ-
> ual unit to a social unit of two or more
> people has certain consequences for a
> therapist. Not only must the therapist
> think in different ways about human
> dilemmas, but he or she must consider
> himself or herself as a member of the
> social unit that contains the problem.
>
> Jay Haley

From a systems framework, the therapist may be seen as a relationship or context therapist. The focus of his or her expertise is on helping people in marriages, families and other social systems relate to each other in ways that are mutually satisfying. From a systems perspective, the therapist does not do individual therapy, that is, try to fix a person. Rather, the therapist interfaces with a person or the context of the person (family) whose symptoms or problems evolved in that context.

Relationship therapy does not preclude working with individuals, or subsystems, or a family, but the interpretive system which guides the therapist's work defines people relatively, rather than substantively. In response to the question, "What kind of person is Joe?" the systems or relationship therapist would place the person in context in his observational schema rather than describing him by means of trait and factor labels which are individually based. That is, "With me the way I was with Joe, he was _____," rather than, "Joe is quiet, anxious and reserved."

From the systems perspective, the therapist would view the family as the primary context, and other systems, such as school, work or church as secondary contexts. In a sense, this distinction between primary and secondary contexts is arbitrary, for the family and other social systems interface with each other in the larger context described by the label suprasystem.

Systems theory is a seminal theory for relationship or contextual therapy in that two of its underlying assumptions are the interrelatedness of people and the belief that symptomatic behavior such as that generally classified as "madness" or "badness" is a logical role given its context. Thus, the individual pathologies that are described by the psychiatric diagnostic nomenclature are considered to be symptomatic of dysfunctional contexts in which the "dysfunctional" role evolved as a system maintenance or system preservation function.

From the logic of the systems model, it follows that arbitrarily designating the family context as the context for treatment ignores the idea that "family pathology" may be symptomatic of the dysfunction of the suprasystem and may serve a system maintenance function in that context. From this same logic, it also follows that the therapist must include him or herself as a part of this system. Indeed, as part of the larger societal system which defines the client's behavior as dysfunctional, the therapist's role may be a part of the problem (Haley, 1976). If we view family pathology apart from the network of social systems of which the family system is a part, then we have merely moved one social unit higher than "individual pathology."

A general goal of family therapy is to help a family context evolve so that symptomatic behavior in an individual is not a necessary role for the continued existence of the system. Community therapy or societal therapy, it would seem, should have a similar goal, i.e., that family pathology as symptomatic behavior is not a functional role. Thus family, community and social therapy are of the same class of activities. We as family, community and social therapists may be construed by our roles as symptomatic. We evolved our roles in the contexts of the systems we seek to change. Therapists might well be viewed as "bad" or "mad" in the same sense as delinquents or phobics. As therapists, we like other people, cannot transcend ourselves. Whatever theories we invent, they are still our own. This same statement might be made for us and our contexts. While we cannot transcend our contexts, we can be aware that from the systems model our role as change agents is a part of the very contexts we seek to change.

While the preceding comments can be construed as an indictment of therapists, it is intended as a logical analysis coming from the systems perspective. For good or ill, a society evolves roles to assure the maintenance of that society. Our role as therapists is merely one such role. Our general charge from the society seems to be to "help people fit," i.e., to be more adaptive to the way we want our society to be. This poses an interesting dilemma from the systems model, for the logic of this model states that that which is called "maladaptive" does fit. Symptomatic behavior is a functional role in the context whether the symptom is "madness" or "badness" in the individual, the family, the community or in the society. Taking this logic one step further, to respond to the charge to "help people (or systems) fit" we in essence can only do this by helping them become misfits--doing behavior that is illogical to their context(s).

One can infer from the systems model that if the societal contexts had evolved processes consistent with the ideals set forth by those societies, then therapy per se would not be a functional role. It would seem that a society evolves the role of therapist only to deal with discrepancies between its ideals and the processes the society activates to attain these ideals. For centuries, people have speculated on both the ideal and the processes by which to attain the ideal. Some have thrown up their hands in despair and have sought to break away from society, as witnessed by the various communitarian and utopian experiments that have been attempted throughout history. People cannot transcend themselves. Whatever theories and societies they invent, they are still their own. Setting forth ideals is not bad per se, but often the ideals we invent are utopian in the sense that the processes we invent are not capable of attaining these ideals. As finite beings, we cannot claim infinite wisdom and our inventions will probably always fall short in comparison to our ideals. We can however, begin to get a closer match between the ideals we pose and the processes we invent to attain these ideals. Let not our methods contradict what we desire. Therapists must seek to use procedures consistent with the ideals set forth by their models of a functional context. The therapist whose processes contradict the attainment of the ideal is akin to the wife who nags as a way of getting more love, or a parent who punishes an adolescent for not being more mature by treating him like a five year old. Perhaps a goal of family therapy is to help families (subsystems of the society) formulate goals which are somewhat less utopian and to evolve processes by means of which these goals are more nearly attainable.

With these introductory remarks let us turn now to a closer look at applications for the therapy process which seem to be consistent with the systems model.

General Principles

Systems theory is viewed as a theory of stability and not a theory of change. The theory describes quite vividly how a system maintains itself. However, a close look at how a system maintains itself or ceases to exist as a system can give some general principles to guide our actions as therapists who must be concerned with change.

The concept of morphostasis implies a near steady-state within the system. The system has feedback processes to maintain the system in this

61

steady-state. The mechanisms of positive and negative feedback are present in families called "functional" as well as "dysfunctional." Thus, whatever a family's current pattern of interaction, it serves to maintain the status quo of the family. Feedback loops from and to each member of the family serve to maintain the feedback loops from and to each member of the family. However painful the experience for family members, there is a certain harmony and security in a given pattern. It fits. It makes sense. It is predictable. The persistence of a pattern and a change in pattern need to be considered together. Two related, useful questions for the family therapist to ask are, "How does this undesirable situation persist?" and, "What is required to change it?" (Watzlawick, Weakland and Fisch, 1974, p. 2).

The systems model is very clear about the appropriate target for change: change the context, maintain this change, and the family system will gradually adapt to this change. A change in context necessitates a change in relationship rules. Thus a family's behavior may be different at a formal dinner than it would be at a picnic. How mother and father relate when alone is different from how they relate when one or more family members or others outside the family are present. A change in one person disrupts the family's usual interaction pattern as well. In effect this change violates the implicit contract about how family members have been with each other and the whole system must seek new, stable patterns of interaction.

Change need not be the only result of this change in person = change in context = change in family proposition. The family may cease to exist as a family. Thus, if one spouse is seen in therapy without the other, and if the client spouse changes, we may find the other spouse maintaining the previous interaction pattern which is the basis for the identity of the relationship and for each person in the relationship. The implicit interpersonal contract would no longer be valid.

In family therapy, the therapist is the person who is different and who by his or her presence comprises the change in context that is the necessary condition for therapeutic change from a systems perspective. The change in context is a here and now phenomenon for the therapeutic session. The therapist must choose his or her own behavior in the face of attempts by the family to have him or her join the family's pattern and thus become part of its usual context. With the therapist who behaves differently the family members may experience, understand or begin to behave differently with each other.

If therapy focuses on a change in the identified patient (I.P.), who is a symptom of the family pattern, without a change in the context of the family, the I.P. may get hooked back into his or her symptomatic behavior.

62

While theoretically the change in the behavior of one person can change the system, the network of relationships, feedback loops, and redundant patterns may be strong enough to offset a change in the I.P.

The problem does not lie within the person from this model; it lies within the system of which the symptomatic behavior is an integral part. The symptomatic behavior is a necessary and logical role in the system. Stated differently, the symptomatic behavior is "dysfunctional" from another framework or model, but within the interpersonal network of the family, it is a logical, sane response, necessary for the maintenance of the system. It is, in effect, adaptive in this dysfunctional context. To focus on changing the individual is to produce behavior that is maladaptive to the family context and thereby threatening to the very existence of the family system. Becoming functional in terms of the more socially acceptable responses defined by mental health models may not make sense given the symptom bearer's context. Attempting to change the one without the other would be akin to asking the I.P. to wear blue jeans to a formal dinner or to show love and affection in the face of hostility. Doing this is not impossible, but by definition, behavior that does not fit the context is "crazy."

The systems model suggests that the roles described in the nomenclature of symptomatic behavior as "madness" or "badness" already fit the context. To request change in symptomatic behavior and to leave the context unchanged, by this same definition, asks the person to become crazy. Thus, the therapeutic goal is a change in context which includes the I.P. The essence of therapy is to create a context in which symptomatic behavior makes no sense. If the symptomatic behavior persists, by definition, the context has not changed.

General principles about intervention in systems therapy with families include the following:

1. A family coming to therapy may express a verbal desire to change. This verbalization may not be useful, for it probably is a part of the family pattern which maintains the status quo. Healthy families probably express no desire to change, but they change spontaneously as appropriate. Stated motivation to change can seduce the therapist into believing that this "motivated" family will change more easily than one that reports resistance to change. However, the dysfunctional family patterns tend to maintain themselves regardless of stated motivation to change. For some family members, there may be an advantage in the dysfunctional pattern. There is always a subsystem that "gets" something from a dysfunctional relationship pattern, and therefore in reciprocity, another subsystem is actively maintaining the pattern.

63

2. The therapist needs to be aware of utopian notions regarding any relationship. Such relationships may look desirable but they are probably not attainable. Total freedom from anxiety, jealousy, fear, worry,and a state of perpetual happiness are decidedly utopian, as is,"We must agree on all things at all times." Utopian notions sensitize people to any slight deviation, which in turn tends to amplify the frequency and extent of the deviations.

3. What you see is not all there is. The family's actual at home behavior is probably tempered by your presence and by the change in the physical setting. There will be, however, sufficient clues as to the nature of the family structure and process to allow the therapist to infer what probably happens in the natural setting.

4. Verbal reports of the presenting problem do not give you an accurate picture of the family situation. However, these verbal reports are quite useful as one hears different reports from different people, giving you a view of each person's interpretive system, primary sensory modalities and metaphors. They are also useful as stimulus events which activate non-verbal and verbal responses from various members of the family.

5. The therapist may find it helpful to try to understand how it feels to be a member of a given family in a general way, as well as how it feels to be each member of that family. How each member feels is related to the meaning he or she gives events that occur in the family and what responses are activated in the family system. The therapist might allow him or herself to flow for a while with the family process in order to get a sense of how it feels to be a part of this context.

6. The therapist will find it useful to attend to how family members attempt to "hook" the therapist and thus form a coalition with him or her. Forming coalitions is a logical strategy in families when one member does not feel sufficiently effective in his or her relationship with another member of the family. Each family member may try to triangulate a third party in an emotional crisis. Thus, "hooking" behavior may be a fairly typical strategy in a given family.

7. Transcending the verbal reports of what the family says it does in response to the symptom bearer, the therapist can predict with reasonable accuracy what the family actually does by being aware of the usual cultural responses to specific symptoms. What is the cultural response to depression, to delinquency, to hyperactivity, to anxiety, to school failure, or to other behavior problems? These logical, cultural responses are probable in most families. The behavior which logically fits the symptom will maintain and escalate the

symptom. It is not different.

8. A family typically comes in for therapy when one member is manifesting symptoms, usually having been labeled bad or sick. Other family members may appear healthy or normal, perhaps more so in contrast to the symptom bearer. The systems therapist must consider how the symptom bearer's problem is useful to the family; what function it serves; what processes get activated around the symptom bearer; what structure or pattern of interaction maintains the symptom bearer in his or her role as well as others in their roles.

9. The therapist may engage one member of the family in conversation, but it is useful to remember when so doing that other family members are listening as well. The therapist has a relationship (converses) with each family member as well as with the system as a whole. You may want to consider in your conversations and interventions what you desire to have other family members hear or observe. What appears to be individual attention in the context of a family can be quite powerful in affecting other family members.

10. Most family members want change without having to change themselves, that is, a unilateral change for that which is a bilateral phenomenon. A good question to ask parents in order to include them in the problem is, "What are you willing to give up in order to achieve the desired behavior from your child?"

11. The concept of morphostasis refers to a system's ability to restore itself according to its own internal structure and operational procedures following any disturbance to the system, whether from within or without. This natural tendency of the family system can be construed as problematic to a therapist who is, by definition, a disturber of the system. Such a natural and healthy tendency of families is a key to the survival of a family, but is often seen as resistance. The therapist must learn to work with this phenomenon rather than creating a problem for the family by asking it to forego a vital survival mechanism. Indeed, it is doubtful that the system can do so consciously. Perhaps the most difficult family for any therapist to work with is the chameleon family whose stability mechanism is its flexibility. That is, the family who appears to be willing to do anything you want is the most powerfully resistant family.

12. From a systems perspective, it is fair to say that a couple marries, not each other, but each other's family system. The intergenerational interaction pattern is part of the marriage contract, however denied or however much the couple may seek to have their relationship be different. In this sense, to be successful in marriage or family therapy may require breaking

a pattern that extends over several generations.

13. As a systems therapist, you may choose to work with the whole family, an extended family network, or with subsystems of the family. But you are not trying to change one or the other alone. You may work with one or the other as a means of changing the system. The purest system position is to relate everything to a relational significance. You are not really interested in the internal thoughts or experiences of the individual, but you may wish to talk with an individual to learn the significance of something in his or her relationships.

14. A basic rule, from the systems perspective, is that as long as the family system keeps interacting around a problem, they will keep the problem. They cannot talk about it unless they have it. Change via systems theory is geared to changing the pattern of the family system. Energy directed toward adaptive behavior not only reduces the energy available for maladaptive behavior, but it also provides energy for the system. It is harder to respond negatively in response to a positive behavior than it is to a negative behavior. The therapist might assist family members in expressing their desires in more functional ways.

15. The substantive content of a conversation is probably not where the problem lies. Families often believe that if issues are talked about and resolved, the problems will disappear. From the systems perspective, however, the problem lies in the communication processes and family structure. But the substantive content can be used to modify or change the communication processes and structures without expressly discussing either.

16. A key to successful therapy with families is helping the members of the family system realize that they are not independent agents. We are free in our internal experiences but not in our interpersonal exchanges. I can manipulate only my half of the behavior. The actions of each affect the other, thus each person shares responsibility for the actions of the other. Unless you the therapist realize this also, you will have a tendency to mislabel.

17. Many marriage and family problems reflect complementary relationship style exchanges. Complementary behaviors are those exchanges which are logically opposite: friendly-shy, dominant-submissive, sloppy-clean, etc. The more complementary the exchanges, the more inflexible the relationship. Symptoms of complementarity are rigidity and tremendous redundancy. Such exchanges can seduce the therapist into seeing victim-persecutor, and control as residing in one person, which leads to mislabeling. From the systems perspective the reciprocal interaction proposition holds that the relationship cannot be maintained as it is unless each continues the complementary role.

The understanding by family members that they cannot not behave and cannot not communicate is essential in marriage and family therapy.

18. Symmetrical relationships describe a competitiveness, which will escalate and ultimately explode, inducing instability. The couple or family members in such a relationship exchange logically similar behaviors. They often see the competitive behavior of the other but do not see themselves as doing similar behavior. A parent who shouts at a child who shouts may not see his or her own behavior as being like that of the child. And if he or she does see it, such behavior may be rationalized on the basis of its having been caused by the other, who shouted first. In an interaction sequence over time, there is no start, although we often isolate one sequence as separate from a previous sequence. "Who started it?" is a misleading and ineffectual question from a systems perspective. It implies linear cause-effect processes. However, reciprocity is the rule. Equifinality describes the continuing nature of the pattern.

19. From a systems perspective, equifinality suggests that the current pattern of interaction within the existing family structure maintains a problem behavior. The therapist, therefore, needs to draw upon a strong background of individual and family developmental theory in order to have a sense of what should be happening that is constructive behavior given the stages which individual members and the family have already attained at a particular point in time. As each member of the family makes functional, constructive moves toward appropriate developmental tasks, the problem person may no longer be so labeled. The problem behavior will no longer fit the context in the evolving structure of the family.

20. A systems therapist must ascertain and decide what are the relevant boundaries of a given family system. All persons living together in a household may constitute one definition. However, other persons may play significant roles in maintaining the status quo in a system. If the problem person has been receiving treatment for the presenting problem from a family physician or another therapist for a period of time, or if a significant relationship with another person, such as a friend, or a brother-in-law has evolved around the problem, the therapist may wish to consider doing the following: He or she may include these persons in therapy and/or seek the input of these persons in attempting to understand the dynamics of the family system. A significant friendship with such a person may be threatened if the problem person gets better. Indeed, it can feel very good to have a "problem" in order to elicit well-intended, sympathetic responses from others. These actions of others can perpetuate a linear cause-effect interpretive system as they reinforce the labels used by others in the family through their particular responses.

21. A major difference between reciprocal and linear cause-effect thinking as regards behavior is reflected in a consideration of whether one asks what behavior preceded another, or whether one is concerned with what behavior caused another. The key to the memory of a behavior is what it occurs relative to. From a systems perspective the memory of a family member's behavior is relative to what preceded it and what followed it. Using linear causality, on the other hand, an ongoing sequence of behavior is arbitrarily divided with one person's behavior being regarded as the cause of the behavior of the other.

22. "Crazy" is doing something that does not make sense to an observer because it cannot be readily explained. However, "crazy" people do not always see themselves as such. "Crazy" or "bad" behavior fits, or makes sense in the context of the system. More specifically, it does not fit the rules of the system to give a kiss in response to nagging, but it is more likely to break the pattern than is anger.

23. We evaluate behavior relative to our utopian notions about what it should be. We all have utopian notions. However, a part of family therapy is to change these notions, many of which are relative to culture. What can a given family be that would be more functional within its culture? Similarly, a therapist must consider whether his or her notions, appropriate in his or her culture, are appropriate for a family in its culture.

24. From a systems perspective, problem behavior can be construed as a plea for help. It means the system is dysfunctional at some level. People with problem behaviors can predict well what will happen in the family, but feel powerless to change what is a self-defeating pattern. They are interwoven into the fabric of the system and are constrained from change attempts that do not fit the rules of the system. "Crazy" or "abnormal" behaviors are thus an attempt to promote change within the rules of the system.

25. Systems theory suggests that we develop an internal model of how others see us and then we project that onto others. When I speak of someone else, I speak of my perception of that person and my belief about their internal motivation. Happy people are those who believe that others are going to treat them kindly. Couples who have a strong bond will have a model that allows them to say, "I didn't like that behavior, but I must be doing something to promote it."

26. In healthy families, choice fulfillment is spread across members. In unhealthy families, choice fulfillment is situated in one or two members. Similarly, in healthy families, all members are dysfunctional sometimes. In unhealthy families, one or two persons have the honor of getting into trouble

all to themselves, helped knowingly or unknowingly by the other family members.

27. Any person can interpret incoming stimuli in different ways if he or she has a flexible interpretive system as opposed to prematurely hardened categories. When family members acquire an alternative explanation or reframe for the behaviors of other family members, different action alternatives become possible. Problem families have almost reflexive responses, based upon their interpretive systems. These responses are not questioned, perhaps because family members do not have the meta-perspective that many interpretations are possible.

28. Family therapy may evolve into parent education or child management training sessions. This probably will not be effective unless one parallels this with parent management training for children. Bilateral change is more likely to effect a more basic systemic change. One can however, use parenting ideas as a means of getting at other aspects of the system, for example, the marital subsystem.

29. A systems therapist helps families develop stable and consistent leadership; define goals and work toward them in constructive ways by encouragement, cooperation, task completion, nurturance and effective handling of crises; have fun together and have each member learn how to contribute to making happy things happen; develop an interpretive system which allows each to see the reciprocal influence process that occurs when people interface; deal effectively with those institutions outside the family which impinge upon it; anticipate developmental tasks and mobilize the family to help members meet them successfully; rear children who have learned to build successful families and thus perhaps help toward building more successful families in the next generation.

30. "Strengths" or "faults" are relative to the interpretive system of the client. A strength in one interpretive system may be a fault in another. Thus, the same behavior may be regarded variously as meticulous, clean, picky, ambitious and dedicated, a symptom of workaholism, strong and silent, or dishonest. No behavior has value independent of the interpretive system which so labels it.

31. The ultimate goal of therapy from a systems perspective is for a couple or family to acquire a more useful epistemology. The fact that a system has requested therapy indicates that the epistemology being used to guide actions and feelings is not effective in achieving desired ends and goals. Thus the goal of the therapist is to modify the structures of the relationships in the system so that a new and more useful set of rules can come into play.

32. A key to successful therapy and to successful relationships is the following: If I am influenced by someone and influence them in turn, I can acquire two kinds of freedom in the relationship. I can make choices about
how I act toward the other person and I can make choices about how I respond to actions by the other person toward me.

Engaging the Family, Assessment and Therapeutic Goals

When does therapy begin? By the time a therapist sees a family, it
probably has already begun. A family with a problem, or with a person identified as having a problem, probably has activated or sought help from others
within the family system and/or from without, i.e. from friends, colleagues,
teachers, ministers, relatives, etc. Thus the family coming in for therapy
probably will already have activated its natural network of resources before
seeking professional assistance. The lack of success from these first therapeutic efforts suggests that the input came from an extended family network
which was part of the same context as the family system. In effect, it did
not comprise a different context, but was already a part of the family context; that is, people who directly or indirectly regularly interface with the
family and have an emotional linkage to the family. Family members often
seek lay therapists who do not constitute a different context. In effect, by
activating its usual network of relationships and staying within its parameters and rules, the context remains the same.

A therapist is a member of the same social context as the family. He or
she is an agent implicitly designated by society to assist people in becoming
more adaptive in accordance with the expectations of society. Thus the
therapist is a peripheral member of the context of the family. The therapist
is certainly not objective in that he or she comes from a different context.
However, the therapist is more peripheral and thus has a lessened emotional
involvement with the family system. Therapists are not "objective" in the
scientific sense, but are subjective relative to their theoretical orientation
and the role of the therapist in the society of which they are a part. These
biases affect the work of the therapist and influence assessment and goal setting activities of the therapy session.

In any case, the therapy has already begun by the time the family con-
tacts the therapist. With the first phone call therapy continues. The request for all household members to come to the therapy session is a start at
redefining the problem as a family or context problem rather than as an individual problem. The therapist's style and manner on the phone sets the tone
for the therapy process, as does the nature of the questions posed by the
therapist. The phone call invites the therapist into the family system. The

therapist begins to evolve a new context for the family.

In the first session, interventions which may be called assessment are part of the therapy. The therapist, as new family member, interfaces with the family, observing, asking questions, listening, making hypothesis testing interventions, etc. The therapist can indirectly intervene into the family under the label of assessment and diagnosis by means of the questions he or she asks. These questions, when not focused on specific prescriptions can creep into a family's consciousness. Such questions and the answers they elicit constitute new input into the family system. For example: Where in your family can you be alone? To whom in your family do you talk to about your problems and successes? How much fun time do you spend with your mom or dad or family? When was the last time you made a funny or surprise thing happen in your family, like putting candles on the table for dinner or bringing home a treat for no reason? In some cases, the answers to these questions are important sources of information. In other cases, the questions can be therapeutic interventions in their own right.

From the outset the therapist interacts with family members in different ways- different from what the family would have the therapist do. For the therapeutic hour, the therapist is a member of the family system. In effect, the therapist as a system joins the family system. But in joining it, it is imperative that the therapist offer a different way to behave from what the family ordinarily does. The therapist must do behavior that is neither the same nor the opposite of what the family is doing.

This "being different" is not limited to any one way to be different. Differentness is relative to context. Dancing at a dance is not different. Dancing at a solemn church ceremony may be different relative to the practices of the church. Differentness is defined here as akin to "craziness," i.e., behavior that does not fit the context. Differentness by definition is doing behavior (creating a context) so family members can be different with one another. To do what is complementary to the family context is, by this definition, neither crazy nor therapeutic. It serves to maintain (with the therapist as a new family member) the existing family context. Any context provides cues as to behavior that is complementary to that context. It is interesting to watch how some families watch for cues (context markers) as to how to be clients in the clinical setting. Therapy-wise clients may begin by giving cues to the therapist as to how he or she should do therapy.

It is typical of families to attempt to hook the therapist into helping the family solve its problems in the way the family has already tried to solve its problems. One can describe this as seeking confirmation for their beliefs and validation of their previous attempts to help themselves. Systemically it is viewed as a morphostatic mechanism. It is often construed as resistance; however, it is an essential mechanism to the survival of the family. For the therapist to do what the family requests, by the above definition, however, is not therapeutic.

Some therapists may be different, "crazy," from the outset (akin to dancing in the therapy session). Most therapists seem to prefer to gradually change the family context by selectively complementing and gradually transforming the family's process. The therapeutic ideas and interventions which we present fit the latter mode rather than the first. Regardless of how the therapist initially engages the family, the therapeutic goal is to create a different context in which stability, flexibility, firmness and nurturance can become a part of the family's pattern.

Assessment is a process which aims at defining the family's pattern or structure. In effect, it is a "this is what's going on" statement. From the systems model, the labels assigned to individuals using the psychiatric diagnostic nomenclature make no sense, i.e., do not logically fit the model. These individual dysfunction diagnoses do make sense if one uses an individual pathology model.

More frequently than not, a single individual is presented as having the problem. It is not unusual to hear from the caller, "Why would you want to see the whole family? It is Joe's problem." If the family has consulted and/ or sought treatment from a person whose theoretical model involves an individual pathology diagnosis, it reinforces the belief that the person who needs to be treated and cured is Joe. "If Joe were okay, all would be well." The individual pathology model seems to be the model of choice for many professionals. It is implicit in the label "mental health." The lay public, having consumed the services of such professionals over many years have fairly well internalized this diagnostic framework.

The practitioner of family therapy who bases his practice on the systems model would more accurately be described as a relationship health, a systems health, a family development, or a family health professional: "Thinking of such symptoms as 'depression' or 'phobia' as a contract between people and therefore adaptive to relationships leads to a new way of thinking about therapy" (Haley, 1976, p.2).

The assessment of family dysfunction is somewhat problematic from the systems model. As noted earlier, the definition of what is dysfunctional depends on criteria from outside the context of the system. From the point of view of a systems perspective, a system which maintains itself evolves roles among its component members to this end. Therefore, in one sense an alcoholic, a depressed person, a delinquent, or a phobic activate feedback loops between family members to maintain the system. However, in the broader society, these roles are viewed as not useful, or as waste products of the family system. A challenge for the family therapist is to help the family maintain itself without these maladaptive roles.

In a general sense, the nature of the presenting problem is not specific as to the pattern of interaction or structure of the family. Whether an IP is called alcoholic, substance abuser, depressed, phobic or delinquent, tells you little about the pattern of interaction which maintains the problem. Systems theory provides no explanation as to the different kinds of maladaptive roles that may emerge in a dysfunctional family context.

Defining a "negative" pattern in a family implies the flip side of the coin, or an inference about what a healthy or "positive" family pattern looks like. While it is useful to know the existing dysfunctional pattern, the therapist's and the family's diagnosis of dysfunction implies that both the therapist and the family have a model in their heads of what a functional family looks like. To a great degree, these models reflect the values of the community and social context of which the family is a member.

Specific family therapies describe functional families in a variety of ways. Our concern is the use of the systems model to derive a picture of a functional family system. A few propositions and related questions from this model are presented below:

1. A system needs to be stable and yet be able to change or to be flexible. How is stability maintained in a given family? How does change occur? Are family interactions consistent, thus providing the security of predictability?

2. Families like individuals go through developmental stages. At what stage is the family? At what stage is each individual member of the family? At what stage did the crisis begin?

3. The family needs to be both open and closed. How open is the family from within and without the system? Under what circumstances and through what processes does it become open to influences or capable of shutting down influences? What value orientation or explanation justifies this decision?

4. Family members need to be individuals and yet feel like they belong. How is individuality respected? How are attempts at inclusion and togetherness handled? Do family members have independence of thoughts, feelings

73

and judgement? Does the family seek to promote giving up a sense of self in favor of the family identity?

5. Communication is feedback and this information exchange is the energy that maintains the system. How much energy is directed toward maintenance functions? Toward task functions? How do family members learn about their behavior? What are the feedback mechanisms in the family? Are messages clear? Ambiguous?

6. A system is composed of subsystems with roles which logically complement each other. Are these roles clear? Are these roles confused and conflicted? Is the parental subsystem marked by clear generational role differences? Do children parent? Do parents rely on children for emotional support? Is the parental subsystem dependent upon grandparents?

Our bias suggests that assessment is most useful when it describes what needs to happen in the family rather than what's wrong with the family. As stated earlier, these are related statements since the flip side of "what's wrong" is the complementary "here is what would be right." The way one thinks about a problem and labels it can crystallize the problem and aid in its persistence. Assessment which helps a family decide a direction for therapy transforms the therapy experience into a developmental process in which the family members learn to be different with one another in the different context created by the therapist.

The following characteristics seem to be keys to the successful functioning of family systems and help define "what would be right" processes:

1. A legitimate source of authority, established and supported over time.

2. A stable rule system established and consistently acted upon.

3. Stable and consistent shares of nurturing behavior.

4. Effective and stable child rearing and marriage maintenance practices.

5. A set of goals toward which the family and each individual works.

6. Sufficient flexibility and adaptability to accomodate normal developmental challenges as well as unexpected crises.

The family's designation of one person as "the problem" may be for purposes of public consumption. Many family members can assess and are aware

74

of other problems which family rules prohibit from sharing publicly. Thus it is important to remember that from a systems perspective the verbal messages about a problem are most helpful as labels or metaphors which provide information regarding interaction patterns within the family system. For example, a child described as a "monster" or as "sensitive" implies relational behaviors that fit these labels. One can infer from such labels the kinds of relationships which exist between parents relative to the child in question.

The systems model focuses on here and now processes as the necessary and sufficient data for assessment (equifinality), and for developmentally suggesting a therapeutic goal. Here and now questions the therapist may find useful in observing the family include the following: How do family members sit relative to one another? Who speaks? To whom? In what sequence? What nonverbal messages do you observe with what specific activities?

Pragmatics

Therapy can be viewed as a process which involves helping the family move, through a series of incremental steps, toward a basic goal : the gradual transformation of the context into one in which symptomatic behavior is no longer a complementary role. In the following section we present ideas and/or specific interventions which might be a part of this information process.

1. Very few families come to therapy with a systems epistemology as part of their implicit or explicit interpretive frames. They may acknowledge that each person affects the other, but they will ask the therapist, directly or indirectly, to join them in their effort to help or change the symptom-bearer, the IP. When an attempt is made to have the family become involved in the problem, they may choose to withdraw from therapy and take the IP to someone who will "help" that family member. As a strategy, the therapist may need to appear to join the family in its efforts to change the symptom-bearer as a means of involving the entire family in what the systems therapist believes is a family problem.

2. A first task in family therapy is to get everyone to become a part of the problem. This need not necessarily be equated with admitting to being a part of the problem. It does mean activating changes in the communication processes or structure of the family, which involves movement by every member: "You tell me that Johnny's hyperactivity is the problem. I wonder how he was selected instead of Joan, for her weight problem; instead of Mom, for her anxiety and feelings of isolation; instead of Dad, for his reluctance to come home to listen to more of the same and become the 'heavy'?"

3. We often view problems as active agents which must be attacked. All we may need to do, however, is to remove inhibitors which prevent improvement or resolution. Human behavior is a stream that needs to be unblocked, not attacked. Any different response other than the logical "attack" may unblock that stream. Systems theory would prescribe activities that may be helpful toward that end rather than describing what is going on. For example, a family with a long history of problems may not have experienced happy events for a long time. A prescription for doing "silly" or "crazy" things may unlock resources for coping with problems.

4. Many families have little to talk about, so they talk about problems. A therapist might help the family enrich its total repertoire of experiences by suggesting that they go to a movie, a play, out to dinner, or visit the zoo, etc., in order to get new inputs into the system and provide something different about which to talk. Self-disclosure by family members also increases the amount of available information in the family.

5. It is important to create conditions within a family in which individual self-esteem is fostered and enhanced. There must be stable, consistent leadership by the parents and an emphasis on constructive behavior. Using these as a foundation a family can then build toward good work habits, coopera- tion, and task completion. In a dysfunctional family, there will be little that is done together. Tasks are not completed. It is likely that the family will not be very well liked by its members. Are there tasks that get done by the family? Is everything done in a haphazard manner? Good feelings and self-esteem come from productivity. If the ability to do things well is not developed, there will be problems.

6. An important rule for the systems therapist is to bring expectations into focus. Ask where family members are going rather than focusing on rule breaking. The problem adolescent cannot be treated with reams of "don'ts" and then put into isolation. He or she must have a goal on which to focus. The emphasis should be on where and how things should go rather than on how things go wrong. The therapist might find out what kind of social obsta- cles the adolescent is involved in overcoming and assist the family in helping him or her. The therapist may, for example, elicit feedforward messages: "What would you like to have happen as a result of your shouting?" The family needs to learn to request desired behavior rather than continuing to criticize the existing undesirable behavior.

7. The absence of negative, destructive elements is not the same as the presence of constructive, positive elements. If you treat a person as s/he is, he or she will remain that way. If you treat him or her as he or she could be, there is an increased possibility for change. The therapist helps the

family recognize that dealing with adolescents effectively requires attention to the things the teen should be. Stopping delinquent behavior through punishment is not the same as generating something creative and useful. The former relates to the person as he or she is; the latter moves toward potential.

8. It may be useful to help family members move from a discussion of a particular topic to a discussion about how they talk with one another, relate to each other, handle problem-solving, make decisions, etc. The topic then becomes analog. They may discuss this topic with some of their same conflictual interpersonal style and it may be helpful to help them learn a constructive way of meta-communicating. This can be done through role-playing, modeling, practicing or having the therapist take the role of the alter ego and coaching family members as they talk.

9. What do family members believe or assume about themselves and others to maintain the behavior that follows logically from their beliefs and sustains their dysfunctional patterns? What other metaphors would help them to make different choices? A therapeutic task may be to provide the family with explanations, or reframes, which provide solutions where their existing interpretive systems do not. Such an alternative explanation probably needs to be of a higher logical order than the family's existing interpretive system. That is, it must transcend the dichotomies currently employed by the family. For example, within a framework which says obedience = good, and disobedience = bad, rebellious behavior by a teenager might be reframed as normal movement toward independence or as serving a function to give mother a role: "Johnny is the last child to look out for you and be sure that you still have a role in the family." To the teenager the reframe might be: "It is really generous of you, as the last child, to look out for mother and be sure that she still has a role in your family." The goal of the reframe is to provide an interpretation that explains the interaction sequence as well as, if not better than, the previous explanation. A new interpretation opens up behavioral alternatives and hopefully precludes existing dysfunctional behaviors.

10. Problem families often get that way because initial crises are not handled well. For example, culturally, we view adolescence as a stormy time. However, many adolescents make it through without problems. On the other hand, if the family is messed up, the adolescents may be too. In adolescence there is a general lack of definition about what could or should be going on. Adolescents are neither children nor adults, and yet they are both at times. Adolescents need constructive goals toward which to work and systems in which opportunities are provided for working toward these goals. A therapist may help the adolescent formulate some goals and help the family to provide the necessary opportunities for working toward them.

11. A therapist can help families learn to give feedforward messages, i.e., request desired behavior rather than criticizing, which logically begets criticism. The therapist can do this by asking individuals what response or behavior they desire when they criticize one another. Families are quite good at relating what they do not like, but often have difficulty describing exactly what they would like to have other family members do. The feedforward process introduces more than a possibly more effective behavior. It also provides vivid descriptions, probably specific and behavioral, about what is desired. Thus the shout in frustration or the criticism, "You never hug me!", becomes, "I would really like a hug."

12. Many problems in families would resolve themselves if it were not for the triangulation process, or the formulation of coalitions in an attempt to gain more power. The intervention of a third party may look like a rescue attempt, but it can also be construed as blocking resolution. For example, two children who fight, often begin to fight less when mom or dad stop intervening to break up fights. The relationship is thus free to seek its own level, to build its own pattern with different responses without the triangulated third party. Similarly, parents might be encouraged to let one another deal with a child rather than becoming the third leg of a triangle.

13. A family therapist might assist a family in learning to think relatively, thus seeing, directly or indirectly, the self and relationship defeating patterns in which each member of the family is engaged. The general rule is that no behavior can be maintained for long on its own energy; it needs a complementary behavior to maintain it. Criticism logically begets and maintains criticism. Shouting logically begets and maintains shouting or withdrawal – a louder form of shouting. As a therapist, you must be aware that the road to change is via a change in context and thus, behavior, the logical response to which is the behavior desired. An empathic, respectful, understanding response in the face of shouting, if maintained, will slowly but surely bring down the shouting. Family members need to learn to choose their own behavior in response to others.

14. Providing families with insight about how their system functions is of questionable value from a systems perspective. Clients will tend to discuss these therapist-given insights using the same dysfunctional patterns they employ to process problematic issues. They will find pieces of the insight to use, or form a coalition with, to justify their position. Thus the substantive explanation is of limited utility in changing behavior. The nature of relationships may need to change, but awareness must be accompanied by a new process. And a new pattern of interaction can be initiated without insight.

15. Change in behavior in a family is no change if it is the opposite of the

problem pattern. A family member, in response to the ineffectiveness of shouting, may withdraw and become silent. This appears to be "different" behavior. However, silence is the opposite identity member of noise (shouting), and withdrawal is the opposite identity member of presence. Thus silent withdrawal is a louder form of shouting and therefore by definition is not "different." To do something different would be for one member of the shouting match to tickle the nose of the other with a feather, thereby stepping out of the linear, logical response pattern.

16. A happy family is one in which happy things happen. A useful consideration is how many things do family members do for fun, and do they always take parenting, marriaging, and familying seriously. Correspondingly, how much time do mom and dad spend doing fun things together as husband and wife, apart from the children? Many couples forget how important it is to be husband and wife as well as parents. Good marriages create a context for functional families.

17. People in dysfunctional relationships pay more attention to analog than to digital communication. This sensitivity to analog often precludes resolution of the issue or problem. For example, if Johnny, upon being told that it is time for bed decides to pout and talk back, and the parent responds with, "Don't talk to me like that," or else pleads with or placates the child, this response to the analog assures its continuation. A response to task or issue, by-passing the analog, probably will be a more functional response. The therapist might help family members focus on issues.

18. A systems therapist realizes that children play off their parents. If parents communicate by their actions that they love each other and their marriage, the children will respond to this. If parents are optimistic, it is likely that the children will also be optimistic. Families that are having difficulties do not communicate optimism and hope. There must be a steadfastness in the application of positive pressure. Problems must be met head on, dealt with effectively, and without blaming. That is, problems are discussed sufficiently to understand what is going on. Then the effort is aimed at finding solutions rather than toward a continued rehashing of the problems.

19. The most frequent type of parent combination in dysfunctional families is a couple composed of one who is weak and one who is strong. This complementarity often creates a spiral effect, which further isolates the parents from each other and makes their treatment of the children even more divergent. The parental coalition needs to be strengthened so that the child is treated according to the child's needs and not according to the parents' needs. Parents must coalesce around their parental rules and discipline and share both nurturing and enforcer functions.

20. Discussions about problems dominate in problem marriages and families and it is very difficult for the members of the troubled system to see what it is not and what they would like it to be. Although very articulate about their problems, they often cannot see or verbalize much else. Such systems lack positive alternatives and they do not see how their behavior is contributing to the problem. What happens is a set of interactions and not individual behavior. What will help the couple or family is a class of behavior which is of a higher logical order and which is neither opposite nor identical to what they have been doing. The therapist may give an insight into what is happening, but systems theory maintains that the change in the interaction pattern is what makes the difference. For example, a husband who withdraws in response to his wife's nagging can be given the interpretation of the nagging as a desire on her part to have him spend more time with her. Her method is contradictory to attaining the desired goal, however, and she can be taught a new, more positive way to achieve her goals. Likewise, her husband can be taught a new response to the nagging which is consistent with the type of relationship desired by both.

21. Quid pro quo, or something for something else negotiations, i.e., "If I do this then I expect you to do that," can be useful in resolving conflict in specific areas of disagreement such as in-laws, money, social behavior, child rearing, etc. When there is an outcome or a task to perform, such negotiations work well. But quid pro quo behavior does not work well with relationship problems: "I'll give you three hugs for two pats on the bottom." If you trade off interpersonal behavior, you are no longer able to be spontaneous. Feeling choice in this area is essential, and the tally chart must be thrown away. Many people acquiesce in doing loving behavior that is requested. However, its having been requested removes the possibility of choice in the matter. And to comply under such conditions results in the feeling, "Yes, but I had to ask you."

22. In a family, the person exercising what looks to be power behavior, i.e., the authoritarian, has the least actual control. In effect, one gets more control by giving control. A strong husband and wife relationship which allows control to shift back and forth gets more control. Control behavior, as manifested in the parallel relationship style, is reciprocally controlling and seems to have built into it the implicit understanding that actual control of a relationship is illusional. Reciprocal control and freedom for both parties are possible when both recognize and accept the reciprocal nature of relationships.

23. In a healthy family system, it is validating for members to see themselves as making choices and thus as being powerful and having an impact on the system. Each family member needs validating experiences, or opportuni-

ties to make decisions which affect the others. If they are not given, they will be taken, often in ways not valued by the family.

24. Families often confuse or mix requests for behavior or performance with the request to feel a certain way. The statement, "I, or you, should feel or should not feel...," is an example of the "be spontaneous" paradox. It is one thing to request performance (take out the garbage), but quite another to request enjoying it (and like it).

25. In a healthy relationship, both parties can entertain two contradictory ideas at the same time. "I can understand the world as you see it and also as I experience it." This requires a meta-perspective of theoretical relativity with the overriding view that there is no "true" explanation (mine) and no "false" explanation (yours).

26. A key part of the learning of a new process is learning to describe relatively or relationally rather than substantively. When you do, I do and I feel, and then you do and you seem to feel, etc., rather than, "You made me mad," or, "If only you would...". This is fundamental to learning to meta-communicate, or learning to talk about how one interacts.

27. In an interaction sequence between family members, a therapist might interrupt to help any member choose a response different from what is characteristic in that sequence and thus maintains it. A different response will break the self-defeating reciprocal pattern. Such different responses may not seem logical to the given event; in fact, they may appear to be "crazy." But they make sense in that they break the pattern and introduce something different. This is one instance in which craziness may be seen as a logical, or sane, response to dysfunctional communication.

28. Many chronic family problems have developed in response to crises, i.e., illness, loss of a job, etc. The crisis occurred and the family adjusted, but when the crisis ended, the pattern was never dropped. For example, father becomes ill. Family adjusts. Mother goes back to work and children assist with family chores. Father gets well, but the "crisis" pattern persists without appropriate adjustments. Such changes in response to crisis can be used to shift a family, as a therapist induces a new "crisis." A therapist may assign a family member the task of developing relationships in other contexts outside the family. New inputs or energy will thus be brought into the system and role changes will be necessitated as that member's behavior changes.

29. As with all living systems, the family's survival is extremely bound up with its external environment. As family members fit the family context, so the family system fits the context of the system of which it is a subsystem.

It must constantly adapt to and/or exert influence upon its environment. Some families feel powerless in the face of environmental pressures. Indeed there are some environmental pressures about which a single family cannot do very much, such as government policies. However, the therapist may find it useful to help families learn to have an impact where possible. How can the work schedules of both parents be modified so that at least one is home with the children and so that both are in the home together for at least a short time if this is an acceptable or desired change?

30. People outside the family unit affect the family and can reinforce its dysfunctional patterns. If a child has a problem doing homework, there will be an additional flow of negative information coming to the family from the school. The systems therapist, making an ecological intervention, would consider calling the teacher and suggesting that instead of only the steady stream of complaints, he or she also try to compliment the child. This would change the nature of the interactions within the family. Other such ecological interventions might include talking with a coach, boss, peers as appropriate, and/or getting these different influence people together independently of the problem person or the family. The key element for which to look is the source of support for the problem person in the face of a network of negative interaction patterns.

One of the criticisms of systems theory is that it does not describe change mechanisms more precisely. One can illustrate such criticism as follows: "Okay, so you change the context and this change in context = change in the individual = change in family. But you do not explain with the precisions of, for example, behavior theory, how such change is to be accomplished."

In a sense, such criticism comes from a reductionistic philosophy of behavioral science, or, break things down into their component parts, learn as much as you can about these components independent of one another, and the total of the bits of information will give us the knowledge we need to understand, predict and control our world. And while criticism coming from a reductionistic framework is legitimate within that framework, it is based upon a set of assumptions different from those underlying systems theory. Systems theory is anti-reductionistic. To study component parts out of the context of other parts is not meaningful, for each is different without the other. Systems theory provides us with a wholistic perspective. And while at one level the systems framework is a meta-theory, at another level, it is also a pragmatic theory which specifies the mechanisms of change in a wholistic way, eschewing reductionism as inconsistent with its basic premises.

Systems theory as a meta-framework is a unifying model, and many traditional therapeutic processes, e.g., analytic, affective, behavioral, and cognitive, are readily accomodated within its parameters. The systems model would describe each such approach as merely one way in which to create a different context for facilitating the transformation of a family system. Thus specific family therapies, such as those of Satir, Whitaker, Bowen, Ackerman, Haley, Patterson, Watzlawick, and others, may draw upon aspects of many of the more traditional therapies. What the family therapists have in common is a meta-perspective of seeing the interrelatedness of people and systems.

Chapter 9

IN CONCLUSION

> Having abandoned the vocabulary of minds and
> other minds and thus of intersubjectivity, hav-
> ing rejected a commitment to a single objective
> reality variously apprehended from a variety of
> subjective viewpoints, our <u>understanding</u> of man
> is changed. What is in question is not merely a
> vocabulary, not merely a set of concepts, but a
> way of comprehending not a single reality, but
> the multiple realities represented by sometimes
> shared, sometimes divergent subject-matters
> and the subjects they serve to identify.
>
> Steven Bartlett

And so the book is finished, and yet it is never finished or complete. Whenever one asserts what one knows, one is already different, having learned from the very assertion of one's knowledge. And we have learned from the preparation of this manuscript, just as we hope that you have learned from reading the fruits of our effort. You were very much with us as we wrote - you the student of social work, family therapy, counseling, counseling psychology, and ministry, as well as you the practitioner involved in working with families. We tried to anticipate your questions and provide answers. But you were a very large and diverse audience and we feel sure there were many questions which you may have which we have left unanswered. However, as stated in the introduction to this book, your challenge is to continue to learn on your own and to develop your own systems perspective if this seems to be a useful model for you in your life and work. It certainly has been useful to us. It continues to challenge us to learn more about disciplines which previously seemed remote from our formal study of people and human behavior.

We have learned that knowledge is not necessarily ordered in the way that college and university departments are organized. The systems perspective as thus developed seeks to be a unifying theory, or meta-theory, which transcends the specific theories in disciplines that without a unifying framework appear separate and distinct.

85

Further, we no longer regard it meaningful to say that a theoretical framework is either true or false. We do not believe that the truth or falseness of a theory can be known to us. We can only evaluate its relative usefulness, relative to the reasons for which we build or adopt a theory.

Finally, we would like to close with what we consider to be a major challenge of a systems perspective. For in the process of writing this book we have become painfully aware of the difficulties involved in using a language system which is premised on linear concepts to describe adequately a model which assumes mutual interaction and contextual relativity. Thus the challenge to all of us who find systems theory a useful map for the territory we would traverse is to define a symbol system consistent with that map, a key that will better enable us to make use of the map. Undoubtedly such a key would also help us to unlock the doors to a greater understanding and knowledge of the territory we describe as family therapy.

REFERENCES

Bartlett, S. Unpublished Manuscript. St. Louis University, St. Louis, Mo., 1977.

Bateson, G. Steps to an ecology of mind. New York: Ballantine, 1972.

Barnhill, L. & Longo, D. Fixation and regression in the family life cycle. Family Process, December 1978, 17, 469-478.

Bender, A. E. Unpublished Manuscript. St. Louis University, St. Louis, Mo., 1976.

Berrien, F. General and social systems. New Brunswick, N. J.: Rutgers University Press, 1968.

Bertalanffy, L. General systems theory. New York: George Braziller, 1968.

Bossard, J. The law of family interaction. American Journal of Sociology, 1945, pp. 292-294.

Brand, S. II Cybernetic frontiers. New York: Random House, 1974.

Bronowski, J. The origins of knowledge and imagination. New Haven & London: Yale University Press, 1978.

Buckley, W. Sociology and modern systems theory. Englewood Cliffs, N. J.: Prentice-Hall, 1967.

Carter, E. & McGoldrick, M. The family life cycle: A framework for family therapy. New York: Gardner, 1980.

Duvall, E. Family development. Philadelphia: Lippincott, 1962.

Erikson, E. H. Childhood & society. New York: W. W. Norton, 1963.

Gibran, K. The prophet. New York: Alfred A. Knopf, 1951.

Guerin, P. (Ed.). Family therapy. New York: Gardner, 1976.

Haley, J. Strategies of psychotherapy. New York: Grune & Stratton, 1963.

Haley, J. Problem-solving therapy. San Francisco: Jossey-Bass, 1976.

Harper, J., Scoresby, A., & Boyce, W. The logical levels of complemen-
tery, symmetrical and parallel interaction classes in family dyads.
Family Process, 1977, 16, 199-210.

Hill, R. & Rodgers, R. H. The developmental approach. In H. Christensen
(Ed.), Handbook of marriage and family therapy. Chicago: Rand
McNally, 1964.

Icheiser, G. Misunderstandings in human relations: A study in false social
perception. American Journal of Sociology, 1949, 54 (5), 400-401.

Kelly, G. The psychology of personal constructs. New York: W. W.
Norton, 1955.

Kuhn, T. The structure of scientific revolutions. Chicago: University of
Chicago Press, 1970.

Laszlo, E. Basic constructs of systems philosophy. Systematics, 1972, 10,
40-54.

Lederer, W. & Jackson, D. The mirages of marriage. New York: W. W.
Norton, 1968.

Malcolm, J. The reporter at large: The one-way mirror. New Yorker,
May 15, 1978, 39-114.

Palazzoli, R., Boscolo, L., Cecchin, G., & Prata, G. Paradox and
counterparadox. New York: Jason Aronson, 1978.

Sadovsky, V. N. Problems of a general systems theory as a meta-theory.
Ratio, June 1974, 33-50.

Scoresby, A. & Christensen, B. Differences in interaction and environmental conditions of client and non-client families: Implications for counse-
lors. Journal of Marriage and Family Counseling, 1976, 2, 63-72.

Seidler, M. Problems of systems epistemology. International Philosophical
Quarterly, 1979, 19, 29-60.

Speer, C. Family systems: Morphogenesis and morphostasis, or is homeostasis enough? Family Process, September 1970, 9 (3), 259-277.

Watts, A. The book: On the taboo against knowing who you are. New York: Pantheon, 1966.

Watzlawick, P. How real is real? New York: Vintage Books, 1976.

Watzlawick, P., Beavin, J., & Jackson, D. Pragmatics of human communication. New York: W. W. Norton, 1974.

Watzlawick, P., Weakland, J., & Fisch, R. Change. New York: W. W. Norton, 1967.

Whitehead, A. N. Science and the modern world. New York: MacMillan, 1926.